UNLOCK YOUR
INTUITION

Unlock Your Intuition

How to Accurately and Reliably Access Your Most Valuable Resource

Andrea Hess

SOUL STAR PUBLISHING

UNLOCK YOUR INTUITION
How to Accurately and Reliable Access Your Most Valuable Resource
United States Copyright, 2007
© Andrea Hess

Published by
Soul Star Publishing
www.SoulStarPublishing.com
Tempe, AZ

Edited by Terra Williams
Cover & Text Design by Adina Cucicov

ISBN 978-0-9796377-0-4
Printed in the United States of America

Acknowledgements

My first thanks goes to my husband Mark for his unconditional love and support. I thank the many clients who have encouraged me in my work and who have allowed me to touch their lives and Souls. You are all an inspiration to me. A special thanks also goes to my teacher and friend, Mamie Wheeler. Without her willingness and openness in sharing her knowledge and expertise, I would have never entered into this incredible profession. My thanks also to my parents and friends who encouraged me on this journey.

My greatest gratitude, however, goes to the Divine Creator and my Guides and teachers in Spirit, who have inspired and guided me on my path.

TABLE OF CONTENTS

PREFACE

S even years ago, I would have told you that all I wanted to do with my life is become an opera singer. I moved to Arizona to pursue my Masters Degree in Opera Performance in 1998, with absolutely no idea that my life was going to take a turn towards the healing arts. I did not perceive myself as psychic by any means—in fact, I did not give matters of spirituality any consideration whatsoever.

The impulse to go to school for massage therapy came a year later. I thought it would be a fun profession that could sustain me in between singing engagements. Without having any idea what I was getting myself into, I started training to become a massage therapist while I was also still taking graduate school classes. The Southwest Institute of Healing Arts offers a very diverse range of energy-based healing modalities as well as massage therapy instruction. I have to confess that I thought many of the people that went around studying Reiki, Polarity, and talking to their Spirit Guides were a little crazy. I didn't know anything about energy work, nor did I really believe in its validity.

Imagine my surprise when I walked away from some of my earliest therapies with tremendous pain in my body. While I wanted to chalk this up to the normal aches and pains that come with a physically demanding job, I soon realized that my pain was directly linked to where my clients were holding distress and tension in their own bodies. Fifteen minutes after a session had ended, I would end up feeling my clients' physical pain in my own body. How could this be?

My massage teachers were quick to tell me: energetic transference. Apparently, I was literally taking on the discordant and painful energies my clients were holding at the physical level. As you might imagine, I changed my mind about energy modalities in a hurry. I took a few classes in Polarity and Reiki myself, and learned how to manage my therapies so that I did not take on the negative or painful energies my clients were holding in their bodies. But I was still reluctant to openly practice any kind of energy work.

One day, I met a friend for coffee. She was very excited about an intuitive reading she had just received. She was determined that I should experience this kind of reading for myself. So I found myself, somewhat reluctantly, scheduling a session with Mamie Wheeler for a Soul Profile reading. It was more money than I should have spent, and I had no idea why I was even going... but I went. The reading blew me away. Not only did the information resonate so deeply with me as accurate, but the energetic clearing opened up whole new realms of opportunity. Did I at this point think this work was something I wanted to do? Goodness, no. I still did not consider myself particularly intuitive. However, the door to the world of spiritual development had blown wide open.

Over the next few years, I studied Vipassana meditation. I also began practicing yoga, and eventually completed yoga teacher training. In a quest to work at a deeper level with my clients, I became a certified Life Coach through Coach for Life in San Diego. I was embracing spirituality in my life personally, but was still uncertain about making it the center of my professional life. As I began building my coaching practice, however, I found myself attracting very spiritual clients over and over again. My coaching sessions became focused on energy and intuition and receiving guidance. When Mamie began offering intuitive practitioner training, I was one of her first students. While I thought that intuitive readings would be another element of my coaching practice, they soon became the core of my work.

This book represents the "how-to" manual I wish I'd had on my path towards accessing my intuition and spiritual resources. Many well-known psychics will tell us that their abilities were obvious at an early age. What is less recognized is that many highly sensitive individuals shut down their intuitive abilities early on in life because of sensory overwhelm, or because the notion of intuition is discredited by parents, caretakers, and teachers. From this place of desensitization, it is often a hard process to reclaim the natural intuitive ability we are blessed with. On my journey, there was a lot of uncertainty and self-doubt, a lot of false starts and wrong turns. I recognize now, of course, that my intuition and inner wisdom was there all along. I simply did not know how to access it reliably and dependably. A lot of guidance had to hit me over the head a few times, sometimes quite painfully, before I recognized it for what it was.

Today, I use my intuition to earn my living, and to make big and small life decisions every single day. It is truly an invaluable resource. So much wisdom and information is available to us, if only we open up to the possibility that we ourselves have all the answers we will ever need. We are miraculously supported by a loving Universe, and our intuition is the resource that can assist us in making the most of this support. I hope that this book will assist you in embracing one of the most invaluable resources at your disposal: your intuition.

ᏋᏰ

CHAPTER ONE

UNLOCK YOUR INTUITION

Y ou've been offered a job. At first glance, it seems like a great opportunity, with a higher salary than you are currently receiving. But lately you've been doing research into starting your own business. This new job would certainly not allow for you to focus on creating a business of your own. You're not sure what to do. So you sit down, take a few deep breaths, and access your intuition. Within seconds, a clear flow of information becomes available to you. The new job is not aligned with your highest path and purpose. While the initial salary boost would be nice, you would end up overworked and unfulfilled. Putting your resources into your own business, however, would lead to the same amount of additional work hours and income within three months. Your business, however, would bring you greater fulfillment, and far more potential income in the long run than this job opportunity. Within six months, a part-time opportunity with your current employer is likely to present itself, allowing you to enjoy health insurance and a steady income while devoting more time to your own business. Within a year, you will most probably be able to make your business your full-time endeavor. Reassured, you turn down the job offer and make the dream of becoming your own boss a reality. Two months later, you sign your first client.

You are ready to buy your first home and leave apartment life behind. You've casually looked at some listings, and now your friend has recommended her realtor to you. But for some reason you find yourself reluctant to call her and start looking for a new home. You take a few quiet minutes out of your day to access your intuition. You realize that buying a home in four months would be a better time frame for you, even though it means going month-to-month on your lease. Your friends all think you're crazy to hesitate, but you hold firm. Three months later, your employer announces that your offices are relocating across town. Homes around your new place of employment are far less expensive, and you are glad not to be stuck with a cross-town commute.

You got a flat tire on your way home last night. You could either go to the tire store first thing this morning, or drive to work on your spare tire and run the errand on your lunch break. You are dreading the idea of having to sit around for an hour or more, waiting on your car. You take a few deep breaths and invite intuitive information to come into your consciousness. It is highly probable that the errand will take far less time in the morning. You follow this guidance, and are in and out of the tire store in fifteen minutes.

Whether we are making life-changing decisions or small everyday choices, the above scenarios are all examples of how our intuition can serve us. Our intuition is one of the most fantastic resources at our disposal. When we are able to access this tool accurately and reliably, it can save us time, money, energy, and a lot of frustration. Our intuition can show us the quickest way towards a desired goal. That goal can be finding a future life partner, or simply getting home in time for dinner. Our intuition can assist us in embracing our life purpose. And our intuition can help us avoid unnecessary detours and roadblocks on our path.

Accuracy and reliability—these two concepts are usually not associated with intuitive information. To most people, intuition is a vague and inconsistent phenomenon that cannot be counted on. To make major life decisions based on intuitive information may seem very risky. If you are reading this, however, you have probably experienced flashes of intuitive insight and clarity. You may have acted on hunches or gut feelings, perhaps with mixed results. You may sometimes feel that more knowledge is waiting for you just at the edge of your consciousness. Perhaps, when you look at your life in hindsight, you recognize the intuitive insight that could have saved you time and difficulties on your path. But your intuition may seem like a fickle thing, inspiring you with accurate insights in one moment, leading you astray the next. You may doubt that you can truly rely upon it as a resource. Or perhaps you feel that you are not intuitively gifted.

Let me put to rest any doubts you may have about your intuitive abilities. Everyone is intuitive. Put aside any concerns you have about being gifted in this area. Your intuition is a function of your Soul itself. Since you most definitely have a Soul, it just becomes a matter of learning how to access and cultivate your inherent intuitive abilities. Your intuition is as much a part of you as your arm or your leg. And, just like your arms and legs, your intuition is available to you to call upon when you need it. After all, you never sit and wait for your arms or legs to move of their own accord, right? When you want to walk across a room, your legs do this for you—because of your intent. You know where you want to go, and your legs take you there. You do not even have to know every detail of how your muscles accomplish this task. You simply create an intention of walking across the room, and your legs are the tools that accomplish this task. This book will teach you how to access intuitive knowledge with the same sure level of dependability and accuracy as your legs respond to your intentions!

Most people unfortunately only turn to their intuition when faced with uncertainty around a major life decision. It becomes a last resort, when reason and logic have yielded no satisfactory solutions to the issue at hand. Without any prior experience in using intuition as a tool, you might want to know whether to enter into or leave a marriage, to quit a career, or to move half-way across the country.

This is a little bit like announcing that you are going to take up running, and you're going to start with a marathon as your first race—next week! Obviously, your body is not conditioned to take on such a challenge. And, most likely, the results of attempting such a race without prior training would be quite painful.

Similarly, starting your intuitive journey in order to solve one of life's really big questions can lead to unhappy results. If you are in a state of mental uncertainty, emotional upheaval, and spiritual unrest, it is unlikely that you will be able to truly receive accurate information when you haven't yet cultivated and trained your intuitive abilities. When you train for a marathon, you begin with running only short distances. Similarly, the best place to start applying your intuition is with life's small choices, where your emotional investment is not so high.

We usually don't give life's small choices much consideration. We tend to do what we feel we have to, what others want us to do, or what we are used to doing. And yet, the majority of our lives are shaped by the small decisions we make every day. Whether we spend our lunch hour browsing in a book store, or having lunch with a friend, can have a profound impact on our lives. Wouldn't it be wonderful to choose to spend our lunch hour in a way that uplifts us and moves us forward on our path of growth and evolution? Wouldn't this change the quality of the rest of our day? Wouldn't we come home in a better mood, and relate differently to our family? Would this perhaps lead to more uplifting interactions and inspiring conversations?

Our intuition offers us the opportunity to bring awareness to the seemingly small choices that shape our life experience. We learn how to tune in to the path that leads to our greatest growth and fulfillment, not just in the long-term, but in our everyday circumstances. When we are secure in receiving accurate intuitive guidance in these mundane, day by day choices, we are ready to rely on our intuition in life's big decisions, also.

You already access your intuition on a daily basis. Whether you know it or not, you tap into guidance from your Higher Self and your Spirit Guides all the time. At the subconscious level, you already have an intimate, familiar relationship with the spiritual guidance and information that is available to you. Just like your subconscious manages routine physical tasks such as walking, it also manages your connection to the spiritual plane. Your Higher Self has shaped much of your life without you even being aware of it. That's why it can be so difficult to bring intuitive information forward into consciousness. The inner voice of your intuition feels so familiar—and alarmingly close to the imagination—that you may doubt the information you receive. The messages from your intuition are subtle, and you're used to getting them all the time.

Your intuition is a gift that is designed to make your life easier. You are not sent into this lifetime without assistance, or a roadmap of your path and purpose. You've just forgotten how to tap into this spiritual resource. Through this book, my hope is to empower you to use your intuition as a tool in everyday life. Your Soul knows why it is here and what it wants to accomplish. This information was not designed to be a mysterious secret from your conscious mind. We were always meant to have access to our Soul's path and purpose for its present incarnation.

In this Earth experiment, our Souls express themselves through our conscious and subconscious minds as well as our physical bodies. Over time, a perception of separation of the Soul and our physical selves has arisen in collective consciousness. This separation is merely a perception. In my readings with my clients, it always becomes obvious how significantly the

Soul shapes each of its incarnations, even though we are not necessarily conscious of its influence.

When we tap into our intuitive resources and into the wisdom of our Soul, we become aware of the connection between the spiritual and physical planes of existence. We access the wealth of spiritual resources that are available to us. After all, we are here so that our Soul can grow and learn. That is its purpose. The life lessons and experiences our has Soul chosen for this lifetime, the knowledge and experiences from past lives, the assistance of our spiritual guides and helpers, our Soul-level gifts and talents—all of these were meant to be available to us. This information was meant to be transparent and freely accessible to us in our physical lifetime. Through your intuition, all of this information is yours for the asking. You deserve to have at your fingertips all this available knowledge, perspective, wisdom and guidance.

Over time, developing an additional perspective on life through intuitive information adds a new level of perception to everyday life. Examining the underlying energies of the events, decisions, and mishaps in our lives allows us to live with greater awareness. Our lives run smoother, and small incidents don't lead to big disasters down the road. Misalignments and energetic roadblocks receive our immediate attention and can be resolved without having to manifest themselves into our lives as truly disruptive or unfortunate events. When we are out of alignment with our Soul's highest path and purpose, we receive immediate notice from our intuition. This is a priceless gift. We don't have to waste time and effort investing ourselves in paths that do not lead to growth and fulfillment. We've probably all wandered down a few dead-end roads in this lifetime. Unfulfilling relationships, careers, or educational programs can all be avoided when we tap into the power of our intuitive wisdom. We can waste a lot of years in this lifetime, doing what seems reasonable, or living according to other people's expectations of us. Have you ever done something just because your parents or friends or spouse thought it would be best for you?

We live in a world that prizes rational thought and logic. We are taught early on to think about the consequences of our actions, to carefully weigh the pros and cons of our decisions. It can be quite scary when we begin basing some of our decisions on the information we receive from our intuition. We like to think of ourselves as rational people. But, when it comes to personal decisions, the rational mind is simply not the most appropriate tool for the job.

Rational decision-making allows us to abdicate a degree of responsibility for the outcome of our choices. Just think of all the unknown factors that the rational mind cannot possibly be aware of. You cannot rationally *know* that your new boss will turn out to be an alcoholic. You cannot *know* that the house you just bought will have ongoing and costly plumbing problems. You cannot *know* that your new dog has a rare genetic disorder and will need expensive medications for the rest of its life. And so basing our decisions on logic and rational thought alone actually allows us to blame some of the consequences of our choices on life simply happening to us.

Now, however, we begin consciously accessing our intuition. Suddenly, more information is available to us. But this level of information also brings with it a higher level of responsibility for the consequences of our choices. We can no longer say *"there's no way I could have known ..."* Reason, logic, and even some of our emotions may tell us that the new job we've been offered is the opportunity of a lifetime. But our intuition tells us clearly that the situation would not align with our highest good. Our intuition may tell us that our highest path and purpose is not what seems the easiest or most logical choice. Our intuition may advocate changes we are not sure we're prepared to make. And often, we are not given the satisfaction of even knowing that we made the right choice. And yet, once we begin to listen to our intuition, it gets louder and louder until it becomes hard to ignore.

Some people in your life may also not appreciate your intuitive decision-making. Your wife may not understand why you don't want to accept the job offer with the big salary. Your friends may question why you suddenly don't want to buy that nice house, after you've already put money in escrow. Your kids may have already fallen in love with that dog!

THE COURAGE TO LIVE INTUITIVELY

Allowing your intuition to contribute to your choices and decisions takes courage. Accessing your intuition makes you highly responsible for the consequences of your choices. Many people prefer to live half-blind because they do not wish to take full responsibility for the outcome of their decisions. It is up to you to decide whether you want to take the blinders off, gain greater perspective, and act on the information you receive. It is pointless to learn how to unlock your intuition if you are not going to put this resource to use in your life.

Sometimes your intuition will serve you by announcing quite clearly what path would not serve you. Perhaps you're familiar with this scenario: You are talking to a friend, co-worker, or family member. In the midst of conversation, you make a commitment. You offer to help with a project. You make plans. Perhaps you even commit to a joint business venture. But as the conversation ends and you are left to your own devices, you begin feeling uneasy. You are suddenly filled with regret over the commitment you made. This is not simply a slight feeling of annoyance or inconvenience. You are truly in discomfort. Your mind, meanwhile, is playing catch-up as you try to come up with plausible excuses and little white lies to get out of the plans you just committed to. Sometimes our conscious mind gets enamored with an idea and makes decisions before our intuition has a chance to weigh in. The mind can be a noisy place, and a conversation can be even noisier! We don't tune in to our intuition until the mental chatter has subsided. It may even take us setting foot on a path before we recognize that it is not appropriate for us. Our mind can get so busy being logical and rational, so in love with a good idea, that it does not even occur to us that *"right"* and *"reasonable"* might not be the same thing. And so we interview for a job, announce a business expansion, or register for a workshop, only to recognize belatedly that our actions do not align with our desired outcomes.

These things happen all the time. The question then is whether we have the courage to be true to ourselves and our inner wisdom. Sometimes, intuitive insight is inconvenient. I once told a friend that I would accompany her on a retreat, only to find myself in utter discomfort at the thought of the upcoming trip. The travel arrangements were ready to be finalized when I had to come clean and back out. In our collective consciousness, being true to our word is held in high regard. We are taught to keep our commitments, to follow through on plans made. But what is our commitment to ourselves? If something feels truly wrong, should we follow through just because we said we would? Or do we make room for our own personal Truth, and allow our intuition to guide us towards our highest path and purpose? In my case, I simply told my friend exactly how uncomfortable I felt, without even trying to rationalize my decision. And, wouldn't you know it, but she had been feeling the same way! She was actually relieved that I cancelled the trip. I can say from personal experience that I have never regretted any decisions I've made based on my intuition. However, I can think back to quite a few instances when I've regretted ignoring my intuitive insights!

When you are in tune with your intuition, you develop an innate sense of what path is right for you. You don't waste your resources on little detours that lead nowhere. You are on a direct path to growth and fulfillment, and life runs more smoothly. Wonderful synchronicities and happy coincidences happen frequently. Doors and windows of opportunity that you may otherwise have missed become obvious. And you no longer pursue the seemingly obvious opportunities that in reality would lead you nowhere. But acting on your intuitive insight does take courage.

DEVELOPING CONSCIOUS CONTROL

I am always amused by the Hollywood version of intuitive insight. On television, mediums are struck by overwhelming visions over their morning coffee, or have vivid and disturbing dreams that are messages from the great beyond. What always strikes me as frustrating is that our poor medium usually has no idea how to interpret these visions. She is not in control of her talent. While very dramatic on the small screen, this makes her talent pretty useless in the real world! Wouldn't it be far more practical to sit down, ask specific questions, and receive reliable answers? Granted, this wouldn't make for very good television, but in real life, the less dramatic version is infinitely more useful.

As an intuitive professional, I wouldn't be able to do my job if I had to wait for intuitive insight to "hit" me. Like everyone else, I have a busy life. I need to be able to sit down and do my work when I have time available. My intuition has to be "on" when I need to complete sessions for my clients. It's not about being in the mood, or being in the right frame of mind. It just has to work! Why shouldn't you, too, be able to sit down when you have time available and questions on your mind, and access the information you both want and need?

In this book, I would like to introduce you to your intuition as a tool that is entirely within your conscious control. We will work on establishing an accurate and reliable system of access that works, whenever and wherever you may need it. When you've worked through the exercises in this book, you will be able to sit down, ask a question, and receive an answer. It really can be that simple. You will decide what information you need, when you need it, and, ultimately of course, what to do with it when you receive it. This book will show you how to develop a clear and reliable system of accessing your intuition, so that it becomes available to you on demand. Imagine yourself as an athlete or musician. These people train and hone their skills until these skills are dependably second-nature. We're going to do the same

—but it won't take you years and years. After all, your subconscious has been receiving intuitive information all along. Now it is just a matter of bringing this information forward into the conscious mind. We will train your conscious, subconscious and Higher Self to work together so that your intuition becomes available to you whenever you need it.

Accessing your intuition accurately and reliably is a skill that does take some practice. Someone who reads a book about running may know a lot about the sport, but still won't be able to make it through a marathon. Your subconscious and conscious minds need to be trained and conditioned to work together to receive information from your Higher Self, just like an athlete trains and conditions his body. You can read this entire manual in one sitting, and learn a lot. You will not be able to quickly, accurately and dependably access your intuition, however, unless you practice. While the initial methodology may seem a little tedious, it is a necessary part of internalizing the process. So, by all means, read through this entire manual and skip through the exercises. Then go back and diligently complete the processes described, in the right order. Do not short-change yourself on practicing the various stages of your intuitive development. You are at all times laying the foundation for the upcoming exercises and chapters. You may request a free workbook at **www.EmpoweredSoul.com/workbook.htm** to assist you in systematically completing all the exercises in this book.

All processes in this book are designed to help you receive accurate and reliable answers from your Higher Self through clear, mindful questioning. You will learn how to ask the most productive questions, and get clear answers. We will use an external method of divination—dowsing or muscle testing—and simple *"yes"* or *"no"* questions to receive information. At first, there will be some limitations to the questions we ask. As you work your way through this book, the quality of information you are able to receive will expand, the process will become quicker, and you will be able to consciously tune in to your intuition whenever and wherever you wish. Regardless of whether the question is simple or complex, the outline of the process will remain the same. You will ask clear, concise questions within your mind —and you will receive accurate and reliable answers.

By the time you've finished with the exercises in this book, you will be able to consciously access your intuition in the blink of an eye. Once you've internalized your intuitive process, it will become second-nature to you. It will be available to you instantly, whether you're in a meditative state or doing the dishes, or standing in line at the grocery store. While it does require some effort, the process of connecting to your intuition is fun, and you will learn a lot about yourself. The wealth of your intuitive and spiritual resources is waiting for you. It's time to unlock your intuition!

CHAPTER TWO

WHAT IS INTUITION?

Intuition is the pathway by which information comes to us from our Higher Self. It is how we receive information that is not based on our conscious knowledge or life experience. I will talk a great deal in this book about your Higher Self. Your Higher Self is your Soul self. It is the ancient, infinitely wise part of you that was created directly from Spirit. Your Higher Self is not limited to this present incarnation. It has access to all your lifetimes, past, present and future. It spans dimensions, time and space. Your Higher Self *is* pure Spirit. It is the source of your intuitive knowledge and guidance.

Our Higher Self has a perspective on the events of our life that is far broader and more encompassing than our own. It can view our current situations and issues through a frame of reference that spans many lifetimes, dimensions, and aspects of time and space. It also can draw upon the wisdom of our Spirit Guides, and can summon even more assistance in the form of spiritual helpers and teachers, should it need to do so. In other words, there is a vast amount information and wisdom to be gained through our Higher Self.

We are in constant contact with our Higher Self, whether we are aware of it or not. It is tempting to view this part of ourselves as separate from our physical selves. It is hard to imagine that such a magnificent resource is truly part of us. But our Higher Self shapes much of our lifetime's experience, every day. It ensures that we attract the learning experiences we selected before our present incarnation. It infuses our personality and our character. Before we were born, it interacted with our developing body to merge part of itself with our physicality. Our Higher Self is the eternal part of us, beyond the physical, mental, and emotional. It is our truest Self.

If the Higher Self is so infinitely wise, can't it step in and prevent us from making choices that do not align with our highest good? Unfortunately, that is not how our physical world works as a place of learning and growth. Once our Soul incarnates, its vital force energy shifts from the spiritual to the physical plane. You can think of our vital force energy as our Divine spark, the energetic essence that allows us to animate a physical body and makes us alive. It is our gift from Spirit—the energy through which we ourselves can acts as the creators of our own experience. When the Soul incarnates into the physical, it chooses this dimension as its school where it grows through choice, followed by consequence. Because the physical plane is our Soul's chosen place of learning, our physical aspect is given the vital force energy through which it can affect change and act as creator.

Through our intentions, conscious and unconscious, we allow our Higher Self to partake of this vital force energy and act on our behalf. This happens most frequently at the unconscious and subconscious levels. We create an intention or a desired outcome, at any level of thought, and our Higher Self taps into the vital force energy of this intention. In this way, it helps create the energetic chain of events on the spiritual planes that eventually result in the manifestation of our desired outcome. The clearer our intention, the more focused the vital force energy behind that intention is, the more effectively our Higher Self can access this energy and act on our behalf.

Our Higher Self will always act on our behalf, whatever choices—unconscious, subconscious, or conscious—we make. Remember, our physical aspect carries the creative vital force energy. Our Higher Self cannot make our choices for us here in the physical. It tries to assist us with guidance and inspiration, but it is our physical aspect that creates through the vital force energy it is gifted with. We can, however, allow our Higher Self to work for us more effectively by specifically and consciously asking for its guidance.

When we consciously ask for guidance, our Higher Self has access to more of our vital force energy than if we set an unconscious intention. This is why prayer is so effective—it is a transfer of vital force energy to our resources on the spiritual plane. When we allow our Higher Self more access to the vital force energy by consciously requesting guidance, it can interact with us much more effectively. By cultivating our intuition consciously, we are empowering our Higher Self to enter into a deeper, more effective relationship with our physical aspect. When we consciously ask our Higher Self for information, we give it access to a high degree of vital force energy, which it can use to strengthen its ability to communicate with us here in the physical. In other words, the more we consciously ask for guidance, the stronger our relationship with our Higher Self becomes.

Even though it allows us to enter into a deeper and more empowered relationship with our Higher Self, using our intuition does not in any way absolve us of responsibility for our choices. After all, we are the ones that must live with the consequences of our decisions here in the physical plane.

Our Higher Self cannot act on our behalf unless we ask it to. The same is true of our Spirit Guides. Only our intent gives our Higher Self access to the vital force energy it needs to take action. And while it is constantly giving us information, whether we listen, act on its guidance, or even acknowledge its existence, is entirely up to us. The power and responsibility of choice remains at all times with us, here on the physical plane. We can, for example, choose to marry a person even though the relationship does not serve our personal or spiritual growth. Our Higher Self may be energetically yelling at us: *"Don't do it!"* The relationship itself has been one of struggle, but we tell ourselves that relationships take work and compromise. Planning the wedding feels more like a hassle than a joy, but we pretend that this is normal. We feel uneasy about the whole event, but we chalk it up to "wedding jitters." The wedding day arrives and we wake up shrouded in gloom. Can our Higher Self stop us from walking down the aisle? No. It has given us all the information it can. The choice is and remains ours to make, here in the physical dimension.

For the most part, unfortunately, our conscious mind tends to ignore our Higher Self. Our conscious mind, let's face it, is very, very busy! Our schedules are more crowded than ever. We all have a lot to do, every day. Our internal dialogue is constant. We are taught nothing of the wisdom and knowledge of our Higher Selves as we grow up. We are taught to base our decision-making on reason and logic, to think things through, to plan ahead carefully. We are taught to make our choices depending on facts. All of these are functions of the conscious mind. We are not taught that we already know all the answers we will ever need on life's journey.

Collectively, we have forgotten how to communicate with our Higher Self from the conscious level. Very few parents—and no schoolteachers I know of—encourage their children to access their intuitive abilities. This is not their fault. They were simply never taught how to do this for themselves. Very few of us have the opportunity to work on tuning in to what our Higher Self is saying. And so the information that our Higher Self is constantly giving us gets lost in the clutter of the conscious mind. We're too busy thinking and reasoning to recognize that we may already have all the answers. And so, slowly but surely, our conscious mind becomes disconnected from our Higher Self. In readings, I always check for the level of communication between my clients' conscious mind and Higher Self. In very few instances are the two 100% connected as they ought to be. Most of my clients are usually 50% - 75% consciously connected to their Higher Self. This means that, as much as half the time, their conscious minds are not able to perceive the information coming from their Higher Self. I even encounter cases where there is no connection between the Higher Self and the conscious mind at all. In such cases, the client usually feels an alarming lack of guidance and purpose in his life.

Connecting to the resource of our Higher Self puts us in a position of power. Through our intuition, we are able to connect to our Divine nature. Throughout history, many organizations and religious institutions have recognized that, when people are able to connect to their Higher Self, they have no need for an external spiritual or moral source of authority. And so, many of these institutions have told us that we cannot create this connection on our own. Over time, our Soul has become a removed concept. We know we have one (and some of us don't even have that certainty), but we don't exactly know what to do with it. Most of us do not have an intimate relationship with our Soul. We've been taught that to aspire to do so is putting ourselves up on a pedestal. We've been told to be meek and humble, to have blind faith, and to follow an external set of rules. Certainly these rules—whatever religious traditions they are a part of—were originally conceived of to assist Souls at a very low level of spiritual development. But humanity has evolved. Our level of consciousness is now such that we can take responsibility for our own spiritual growth. It is time for us to tap into the full wealth of our spiritual resources.

To access our Higher Self means knowing the plan and purpose of our Soul for this lifetime. We do not have to putter around in the dark, without a lesson plan or curriculum for our growth and learning. This information is available to us, as long as we know how to ask for it. Our Higher Self, meanwhile, tries to be as helpful as it can, given that our conscious minds are so preoccupied. Our Higher Self cannot reach our conscious mind unless we open up to this communication with our intention, our will. It does, however, also have the opportunity to reach us by connecting to our subconscious mind.

Our subconscious mind is usually more connected to our Higher Self than our conscious mind. In readings, I usually find that the subconscious mind holds a 20%–30% greater connection to the Higher Self than the conscious mind. Our subconscious mind is far more open and impressionable than our conscious mind. Because our conscious mind is so busy, our Higher Self often has a much easier time reaching the subconscious. It is through our subconscious that we get gut feelings. It is also how we receive intuitive information in dreams—although not all dreams contain intuitive information. The problem with this method of communication, however, is that the subconscious is capricious. It is about as reliable as a two-year old. The subconscious has only limited reasoning power and cannot distinguish between valuable information and random input. It is full of emotion and memories. This is why we get our precious moments of gut instinct, our flashes of clarity, at random. Because the subconscious is difficult to control, we receive intuitive information not by choice, but by chance. We are not in charge of what we are receiving, or when we are receiving it.

Sometimes we also receive information that looks like an intuitive hit but is actually simply information generated by the subconscious. This is why our gut feelings sometimes send us running in the wrong direction. This makes us doubt our instincts altogether, and so we once again turn to the conscious mind as a more reliable source of information. The cycle of disconnection from our Higher Self then continues, and we stop thinking of ourselves as intuitive beings.

CAN INTUITION BE LEARNED?

Absolutely! All we need to do is create an avenue of conscious access to our Higher Self. Our Higher Self is a willing and happy partner in this process. It has been trying to make its information and insight available to us all along. Our Soul wants to express itself fully in this lifetime. It wants us to consciously know its path and purpose.

Besides our Higher Self, our subconscious mind is going to be a great resource in accessing our intuition also. It will become an ally in this process. While the subconscious is unreliable when left to its own devices, there is one incredibly useful aspect of it that we will exploit to the fullest. The subconscious is made highly impressionable through ritual and repetition. It can be trained! Think of all the activities our subconscious regulates because we've practiced them—activities such as walking, talking, driving, typing, playing a musical instrument, and so on. At first, all these skills took a great deal of concentration and conscious effort. But with practice and repetition, our subconscious reliably took over many of these functions. It will be the same with accessing our intuition—it may take a few sessions, but with practice, our subconscious will internalize the process and reliably handle the mechanics of it all. Don't forget that it has been communicating with our Higher Self all along. The subconscious already knows how to receive information from our Higher Self. It may not have shared all this information with our conscious mind, because we have not yet trained it to do so. But it is accustomed to receiving the information we're after.

Your conscious mind probably needs a little more convincing. It is used to dealing with what it *knows*. Everything else will likely be written off as imagination. Your conscious mind will doubt that the information it receives is truly intuitive. In the beginning, the conscious mind is really going to be more of a hindrance than help to you. You will second-guess yourself. You will wonder whether you are imagining things. You may even think that all this dowsing and muscle-testing is a bunch of hocus-pocus. How could such methods actually work? Be prepared for the objections of the conscious mind. It is simply doing its job—thinking, analyzing, questioning. Doubts are perfectly normal. Let them arise, acknowledge them, and do the exercises in this book anyway!

Your conscious mind will slowly learn how to be receptive to information from your Higher Self. As you practice the exercises in this manual, you will become more and more consciously attuned to what your intuition feels like. You will slowly recognize the validity of the information you receive as you become more practiced in accessing your intuition.Your conscious mind will become a discerning expert in knowing what questions to ask next, and to structure your questions accurately and appropriately. Eventually, your Higher Self, your subconscious and your conscious mind are going to work as a well-coordinated team to give you full access to your intuitive resources.

CONNECTING TO YOUR HIGHER SELF

Before we can begin on our journey of intuitive development, we must be sure that your conscious mind, your subconscious mind, and your Higher Self are all accessible to each other. We must re-establish clear lines of connection to your Higher Self.

This first process is immensely important. Do not skip past this process, or you will undermine all of your efforts within the rest of this book. If you are not connected fully to your Higher Self, you cannot access its knowledge and wisdom. Your intuitive abilities will remain inconsistent. I cannot over-emphasize the importance of this very first step! Imagine if you are placing a phone call, but your phone line has been disconnected. You can dial all you want, but in the end, you are still going to have a very one-sided conversation. Your first step is to re-establish a working *"phone line"* between your conscious, your subconscious, and your Higher Self—and that's exactly what this process is designed to do.

EXERCISE

Repeat the following for five days in a row, without skipping any days. If you miss a day, please start over.

Light a white candle. Then focus your energy with the following breathing pattern:

Breathe in to the count of four, hold for the count of four, exhale to the count of eight. Repeat twice more for a total of three counted breaths.

Then read the following out loud.

"Divine Creator, Divine Agents of Creation and Archangels, my Higher Self, my Spirit Guides, Teachers and Angels... (repeat each name three times).

Acknowledging the totality of my Being on all dimensional and energetic planes of existence, throughout time, I request the following on all subconscious, conscious and higher levels of my existence:

Create a clear channel of communication and manifestation between my subconscious, conscious and Higher Self. Ensure that the subconscious, conscious, and superconscious are 100% connected and in perfect alignment, at all times working together in cooperation towards my highest path and purpose.

For my highest good and the highest good of all, I command this intention to be carried out with joy. Thank you, thank you, thank you."

The conscious mind gets involved in reading the request out loud. Be mindful of the intent of the request as you complete this process—don't just read the words without giving them meaning. In this way, you are making the conscious mind accessible to your Higher Self, and creating an open connection between the two.

Within this process, we add the elements of ritual and repetition in order to target the subconscious mind. Remember how impressionable the subconscious mind is through repeated and consistent practice.

Lastly, notice that we are calling upon spiritual assistance to re-establish the lines of communication for us. Your Guides and your Higher Self know how to activate the "phone line." They are the ones that are actually going to do the work for us. But, just as the phone company will not activate your service without your conscious request, your Guides and Higher Self also cannot act on your behalf without you asking for their assistance. Remember that the power of choice lies entirely within the conscious mind. Through your intent, you are allowing your Higher Self and Guides to access your vital force energy on your behalf. Think of it as placing a "work order" for your helpers on the spiritual plane.

When your conscious mind decided to disconnect from the Higher Self, there was little your Higher Self could do about it. That is the unfortunate aspect of the power of the conscious mind. Luckily, the opposite is also true. When you decide to reactive this connection, your Higher Self will make itself available to you. You may not know exactly how this process functions, just as you do not really know the details of exactly how your phone works. Don't get caught up in doubt because of this. Your Higher Self and your Spirit Guides are the experts of creating open lines of communications with your conscious and subconscious mind, just like the phone company is the expert for setting up your phone service. All you need to do is make the decision to re-establish the lines of communication—and inform the appropriate experts of your decision. This first process will re-establish communication between your Higher Self, conscious and subconscious minds.

Please complete this process before you begin the next step in your intuitive development! Without a complete connection to your Higher Self, you cannot be assured that the information you receive in upcoming exercises isn't simply a product of your subconscious mind.

Depending on your current level of connection to your Higher Self, this process alone may create a profound shift in your life. If you were previously very disconnected from your Higher Self, you may, over the next few weeks, feel a strong sense of purpose and direction in your life. You may experience yourself more as a spiritual being in a physical experience. You may feel a deeper connection to your own Divine origins. Your Higher Self, once it can fully connect with your conscious mind, will immediately work on providing you with information about your highest path and purpose. Make a note of any strong instincts that suddenly arise, and enjoy your new-found connection to your Higher Self.

CHAPTER THREE

DIVINATION
BASICS

N ow that we are fully connected to our Higher Self, we are ready to begin tapping into the information it offers us. The way we begin doing this is through some very simple methods of divination.

Divination is the practice of receiving information from the spiritual plane through an external medium. The tarot, astrology, runes, dowsing, angel cards, the I Ching, palm reading, muscle testing, tea leaves, and an endless number of other techniques have all served as methods of divination. While I don't dispute the validity of any of these methods, many of them leave a lot of room for interpretation by the reader. When you are just starting out, clarity is essential. We don't want to give the conscious mind any more reason for doubt than it already has.

We are going to begin accessing our intuition through dowsing or muscle testing. What is wonderful about both dowsing and muscle-testing is that you get only two possible answers: yes and no. That's pretty clear!

DOWSING BASICS

In dowsing, we use a pendulum to receive intuitive answers to our questions. Depending on its programming, the pendulum will give us the answers by swinging in certain directions to tell us *"yes," "no,"* or *"undecided."* I personally have a strong preference for dowsing. I love my pendulum, and usually use it to confirm the accuracy of my readings. Because I've been dowsing for a long time, just picking up my pendulum puts me into a receptive, meditative state. Dowsing does involve purchasing a pendulum, as well as clearing and programming it before its first use. Most metaphysical bookstores carry pendulums. If you already own a pendulum, please be sure to take the following steps, even if you've been using it for some time.

CLEARING

Before you begin using your pendulum for dowsing, you must clear it energetically. Pendulums can accumulate energetic residue from their surroundings. You don't know where your pendulum has been, who has handled it, or maybe even used it to dowse. There are several effective ways to clear your pendulum. Choose one of the following methods of clearing.

1) Place the pendulum in a dish of sea salt overnight. Do not add water. Just place the pendulum directly on the salt granules. The salt will absorb all energetic residue from the pendulum. Ordinary table salt will not do the job!

2) Place the pendulum on the soil at the base of a plant, either indoors or in your garden. The plant's energy field will clear any energetic residue from the pendulum for you. The earth will also serve to absorb excess energy.

3) Wash the pendulum in hot, then in cold running water. Repeat this process three times.

All three of these options are equally effective. I tend to have sea salt on hand for its energy-clearing properties, so this is my own preferred method.

PROGRAMMING

Before we start dowsing, your pendulum needs to be programmed so that you know how your subconscious wishes to indicate a *"yes"* or *"no"* or *"maybe"* answer. Once the pendulum is programmed, it will always indicate its answers the same way until you consciously clear its programming. Because you are programming your pendulum specifically for your own personal use, it is not advisable to allow another person to use your pendulum for dowsing.

EXERCISE

Hold the pendulum in your hands and create a surcharge of vital force. Do this by inhaling slowly to the count of four, holding the breath to the count of four, and exhaling slowly to the count of eight. Repeat this breath for a total of three times. Then program the pendulum by saying:

"Divine Creator, Divine Agents of Creation and Archangels (x3), my Higher Self (x3), my Spirit Guides, Teachers and Angels (x3)…

In the name of Divine Truth, Light and Love, I place the intention on this pendulum that it relay all information exclusively from my Higher Self unless I give specific permission that it be otherwise. Let all information align with Divine Truth and be for my Highest Good and the Good of all Beings everywhere. I command that this intention be carried out with joy. Thank you, thank you, thank you."

Now it is time to program your pendulum's answers. Hold your pendulum by its chain and say:

"Please indicate 'Yes'."

The pendulum will swing one way or another. It may be clockwise, counter-clockwise, back and forth, or side to side. Those are the four possible directions. Traditionally, a *"yes"* is a clock-wise circle. Make a note of what the pendulum does—this will be your *"yes"* answer from now on. Once you have gotten a clear indication, say *"Thank you."* This is a good habit to get into after receiving an answer. It lets your Higher Self know that you have consciously received the information and are ready to move on.

"Please indicate 'No'."

Again, the pendulum will swing a certain way. Traditionally, this is a counter-clockwise swing. Make a note of the response and reply with a *"Thank you."*

"Please indicate 'Undecided'."

Sometimes the pendulum will not swing at all. For me, this answer is an odd quivering of the chain. However, there should be some indication here. Again, reply with a *"Thank you."*

MUSCLE TESTING – AN EXCELLENT ALTERNATIVE

In muscle testing, we use our own body to tell us the *"yes"* or *"no"* answer to a question. This process is traditionally done with a partner. The inquirer holds an arm straight out, while their partner applies light downward pressure with two fingers at the wrist of the outstretched arm. The inquirer resists this downward pressure. When the answer to a question is *"no,"* the inquirer's arm will become weak and unable to resist the downward pressure the partner is exerting. When the answer to a question is *"yes,"* the arm will remain firm. While muscle testing is usually done with a partner, we will be amending this methodology so that it can be done by one person alone. For our purposes, working with a partner simply isn't going to be convenient. Sometimes a partner simply isn't going to be available. And you may well want some of the questions you ask—and their answers—to be private. David R. Hawkins describes a wonderful process for muscle testing by one person alone in his book *'Power vs. Force:'*

> *"*... people are able to get good results just by themselves by making an "O" ring with their thumb and forefinger. When the results are *"true,"* the "O" is strong and it's difficult to pull the thumb and forefinger apart; a *"no"* makes them relatively weak and easy to separate.*"*

This is a great methodology that I've used when my pendulum wasn't available to me. I absolutely love the simplicity and effectiveness of this process. Because you are using your own body as a divination device, there is obviously no clearing process that needs to be done before you start. Because I have a personal preference for dowsing, I will not be referring to muscle-testing as frequently within the pages of this book. Please know, however, that you can always substitute this technique for dowsing with a pendulum.

PUTTING YOUR DOUBTS TO REST

Just in case your conscious mind is raising any objections at this point, let me tell you exactly how and why these methods work. Remember how I said we were going to initially focus on the connection between the subconscious and the Higher Self? Dowsing and muscle testing both take full advantage of this connection. There is no hocus-pocus here. When you dowse or muscle test, your Higher Self will connect to your subconscious and give it the answer to your question. The subconscious then gives your body the subtle signals that become a *"yes"* or *"no"* answer.

In dowsing, your subconscious actually creates the movement of the pendulum you are using. Consciously, you will not be aware of creating the movement of the pendulum. It really is a wonderful thing to watch your pendulum seemingly swinging of its own accord! You think you are holding your hand still, but in truth, your subconscious is directing the subtle movements that create the swing of the pendulum.

Similarly, you will not be able to keep your muscles strong if a *"no"* answer is given in muscle-testing. This is what makes these methods so reliable, providing that you are connected to your Higher Self. All the doubts and misgivings of the conscious mind are circumvented. Your conscious mind will simply ask questions and receive the *"yes"* or *"no"* answers. Even if you have a great deal of doubt in your mind, this process still works accurately, because the answers are coming from your Higher Self through your subconscious. Your conscious mind can carry on with its misgivings, reservations and skepticisms. It won't influence the answers at all.

If you have previously tried one or both of these divination methods with mixed results, please be reassured. Both methods are so deceptively simple that they are often done incorrectly. A lot of frustration and misinformation can be the result. We have included programming into our technique that will ensure that the answers are indeed coming from our Higher Self. If you've tried dowsing or muscle testing without such programming, your answers would have mostly come from your subconscious mind, and would have been understandably inconsistent.

THE CONSCIOUS OVERRIDE

Every once in a while, I receive an excited call from a student. *"I can control the movements of my pendulum with my mind!"* they tell me. Of course they can, and so can you.

The conscious mind is at all times able to override the workings of the subconscious. The subconscious mind is instinctive and habitual. It is the very primitive part of us that can be conditioned and trained. It also keeps us safe. When people jump out of airplanes for fun, for example, they are overriding their subconscious. The subconscious mind is signaling fear, because jumping from great heights is likely to kill us. But the conscious mind understands the concept of a parachute and overrides the message from the subconscious mind with reason and logic.

If you are completely determined to receive a *"yes"* or *"no"* in these processes and are actively working to influence the answers, you will override your subconscious mind through your conscious will. You can manipulate your pendulum with your mind—but you do have to do so consciously.

Will this compromise your accuracy? Not unless you're actively trying to receive a particular answer, or are determined to receive no answer at all. Divination works best when the conscious mind is relaxed, open, and receptive. You can have doubts and misgivings, and the process will still work perfectly. But if you are actively working against the divination method you have chosen, your conscious mind will override the signals of your subconscious, and you will manipulate the answers you receive, or receive no information at all.

ENSURING ACCURACY

Before you start with your method of divination, it is imperative that we create a consistent process to start each session. With this process, we will essentially "log on" to our Higher Self. You will use this process each and every time you pick up your pendulum, or muscle test. It will be tempting, when a question pops into your head, to simply pick up your pendulum or link your fingers without going through this preparation process. Without an appropriate process, you simply cannot be sure of where your answers are coming from. Instead of coming from your Higher Self, the answers may simply arise from your subconscious. The intention of this log-on process is of tremendous importance, especially at the start of your journey of intuitive development. For each and every session, you must set the intention that all your answers come from your Higher Self. This is how you ensure that you are truly receiving insight and information from this source. Always be mindful of where you want your answers coming from.

Remember also how susceptible the subconscious is to ritual and repetition. We are going to continue to put these traits to good use. There will be days when you are tired, unfocused, or in emotional turmoil. Practicing a consistent process now will allow you to receive dependable information later on, even under less than ideal circumstances.

Think of this initial log-on process as a safety device to ensure the accuracy of the information you receive. Please don't short-change yourself by skipping this step when you practice divination. Establishing confidence early on in your intuitive development is so important. There is nothing more powerful or uplifting than knowing that you can fully rely on your intuition. We are starting out very simply with *"yes"* or *"no"* questions. But we are going to greatly expand from here, and laying a foundation of confidence and accuracy will greatly serve you as you move through this manual. *So use this process every single time you access your intuition!*

PROCESS

Create a surcharge of vital force. Do this by inhaling slowly to the count of four, holding the breath to the count of four, and exhaling slowly to the count of eight. Repeat this breath for a total of three times. Then say:

> *"In the name of Divine Truth, Love and Light, let all information come from my Higher Self, in alignment with Divine Truth for my Highest Good and the Highest Good of all Beings everywhere. Thank you, thank you, thank you."*

Let's talk briefly about the intention we are creating through this simple process. We are asking all information to come from your Higher Self, rather than any other source. Even if you are later on communicating with your Spirit Guides or other entities, your Higher Self should still relay their information to you.

We are also determining that all information be aligned with Divine Truth. Divine Truth is based on Universal Law. It is spiritual Truth, not the subjective truth based on individual opinions that we often encounter in the physical world. Divine Truth is the energy that allows us to recognize what is right and wrong for ourselves, without judgment. Divine Truth allows for many perspectives and teachings, without absolutes. Divine Truth can come in many different frames of reference. When we are in alignment with Divine Truth, we can stand firmly in our own Truth, without the need to defend it or judge others. When we ask for our information to be aligned with Divine Truth, we are asking for our own personal Truth that serves our highest good. This ensures the quality of the information you receive. Lastly, we ask that all information be in our highest good and the highest good of all beings everywhere. We want the answers we receive to uplift us and to add to our growth and learning. We also want the information to contribute to the continuing spiritual evolution of our whole planet. With this intention, we place our intuition into the service of Spirit.

INTERFERENCE ENERGIES

From time to time, negative energies in our environment can significantly interfere with the divination process. If you consistently receive truly conflicting answers in the upcoming exercises, turn towards the *"Resolving Inconsistencies"* chapter of this book for possible ways to resolve these issues.

GETTING STARTED

You're ready to get started! If you are, at this point, tempted to question your Higher Self about all kinds of things that may be on your mind, please be patient. Probably one of the most difficult aspects of dowsing is to know which questions to ask. It's a little overwhelming to have all the information from your Higher Self available to you—especially when you have to receive this information through carefully worded *"yes"* or *"no"* questions. Knowing how to phrase questions appropriately is a key component in the art of divination. Without the appropriate questions, you may start receiving misinformation and conflicting answers right at the beginning of your journey.

The following exercises are designed to introduce you to the divination process. Through the rest of this chapter and the next, you will learn how to phrase questions in a way that will yield reliable, accurate information from your Higher Self. If you wish, you may download the free companion workbook to all exercises in this book at **http://www.EmpoweredSoul.com/workbook.htm.**

EXERCISE 1

Let's start with a very simple exercise that will give you some insight about yourself.

Take the following areas of your life: *Profession, Finances, Physical Well-Being, Intimate Relationships, Friendships, Family, Personal Development, Spiritual Development, Physical Surroundings, Rest and Relaxation.*

Now ask the following question for each life area:

> ⟡ *Am I fully expressing my Soul's highest path and purpose in the life area of...?*

Please note that in all likelihood, these answers will not surprise you much—and they shouldn't. When you are expressing your Soul's highest path and purpose into any given area of your life, you will find that this life area brings you a great deal of fulfillment. The answer will most likely be *"no"* if you do not feel a very high level of fulfillment in this aspect of your life.

Whenever the answer to the above question is *"no,"* you have the opportunity to venture into the wonderful world of percentages. Percentages allow us to go from the black-and-white realm of *"yes"* and *"no"* into a more detailed, informative picture of the situation. After all, if you find that you are not expressing your Soul's highest path and purpose in the life area of, say, your profession, then it is very reassuring to find out that you are nevertheless 75% of the way there. This gives the information a very different quality than if you had simply received a *"no."*

When asking for percentages, I always advise starting with the half-way mark of 50%. Simply ask:

⬧ *To what percentage am I expressing my Soul's highest path and purpose in this area of my life? More than 50%?*

Depending on the answer you get—let's say in this case it's a *"yes"*—you can proceed with *"Is it more than 60%?"* and on upward until you receive a *"no."* Let's say you find your percentage is between 60% and 70%. You can then continue with *"Is it more than 65%?"*—again, utilizing the half-way mark between the two numbers as a starting point. Then you can then continue your questioning until you receive a *"yes"* for the exact number. While this is a somewhat tedious process in the beginning, it's a great way for you to get comfortable with your method of divination.

Notice how your conscious mind is reacting to this exercise. It may be voicing lots of doubts right about now. That's fine! Allow yourself to notice these thoughts of doubt without reacting to them.

Notice also how your awareness has shifted with this exercise. You already knew to about what level you were expressing your Soul's highest path and purpose in each area by the level of fulfillment you've been experiencing. But how does having a precise percentage shift your awareness? How does it feel to have your level of fulfillment, or lack thereof, validated this way? You may have sensed that your finances were out of alignment with your highest path and purpose. But having this feeling confirmed by your Higher Self may suddenly motivate you to ask for a raise or open that retirement account you've been thinking about.

Later on in this book, you will learn how to ask open-ended questions in order to learn why you may not be fully aligned with your highest path and purpose in any given life area, and how to correct this misalignment. For now, however, this exercise should allow you to experience the accuracy of your divination method, since the answers will reflect your current life circumstances.

EXERCISE 2

The following exercise will probably yield some information you were not consciously aware of. Some of the answer may even surprise you—although, on closer examination, you will find their validity reflected in your life.

There are five major universal energy streams that we, as evolving Souls, must align with in order to experience a high level of fulfillment. These are the universal energies of *Divine Love, Light, Truth, Abundance, and Power.* We all have access to these energy streams. As evolving Souls, these energies are woven into the very fabric of our beings. We must continually align and re-align to receive these energies in order to experience wholeness and fulfillment in all areas of our lives. When we are not in alignment with these energies, we invariably feel stuck or stunted to some degree in moving towards our highest path and purpose. When we create our lives outside of these divine energy streams, our creation inevitably ends up missing something.

Let's use this information to further explore the results of Exercise I. Have a look at the life areas in which you were not fully aligned with your highest path and purpose. When we are out of alignment with our highest path and purpose, we are usually also disconnected from one or more of the divine universal energy streams in that area of our lives.

We can gain more information about the life areas in which we are not fully aligned with our highest path and purpose by asking the following:

◈ *In the life area of ..., am I fully aligned with the universal energy of Divine Love?*

◈ *In the life area of ..., am I fully aligned with the universal energy of Divine Truth?*

◈ *In the life area of ..., am I fully aligned with the universal energy of Divine Light?*

◈ *In the life area of ..., am I fully aligned with the universal energy of Divine Power?*

◈ *In the life area of ..., am I fully aligned with the universal energy of Divine Abundance?*

Wherever you receive a *"no,"* you can once again receive a higher level of detailed information by dowsing for percentages:

◈ *To what percentage am I aligned with the universal energy of Divine ... in this life area? Is it more than 50%?*

You will undoubtedly find that you are out of alignment with one—or even all!—of the universal energy streams in the life areas in which you are not fully aligned with your highest path and purpose. The two misalignments generally go hand in hand. For example, if you are not aligned with your highest path and purpose in the life area of finance because you've not asked for the raise you deserve, you most likely will also be out of alignment with Divine Abundance in this area. This information tells you which energies need to be increased in order for you to align with your highest path and purpose!

Here are detailed descriptions of the divine universal energy streams, how a misalignment may manifest itself, and what methods can be used to re-align to each divine universal energy stream.

DIVINE LOVE

Divine Love is the energy from which all Creation springs. Our Souls were birthed from the desire of Creator Source to experience its own infinite diversity through us, as separate pieces of itself. At the center of Divine Love stands our relationship with ourselves. We, too, create our lives to experience ourselves more fully within different life circumstances. This is how we grow. At the heart of this desire to create is self-love. If we do not love ourselves, why would we create ever new and (hopefully!) more wonderful life circumstances to experience ourselves in?

A misalignment to Divine Love usually reflects as a lack of self-love. We neglect our own needs. There is a lack of self-care. Self-criticism, negative self-talk, or a feeling of being undeserving may arise. We may experience guilt over taking care of ourselves and focus excessively on the needs of others. Eventually, our lack of love for ourselves may be reflected in feeling unloved and unappreciated by others.

We realign to Divine Love by putting our relationship with ourselves first. We practice excellent self-nurture and self-care. We offer ourselves opportunities for fun, fulfillment, and joy. We practice saying *"no"* rather than insisting on sacrificing our own needs. Over time, our improved relationship with ourselves will be reflected in improved external relationships.

DIVINE LIGHT

Divine Light is the energy that brings awareness of Spirit into our lives. When we are in alignment with Divine Light, we know that there is more to us than our conscious and subconscious minds. We understand that we are greater than our present physical incarnation. We have an awareness of a connection to Source and all other living things.Divine Light allows us to be aware of ourselves as spiritual beings in a physical experience. It is through Divine Light that we experience our own divinity.

When we are out of alignment with Divine Light, we tend to focus on the physical plane. We embrace logic and reason. We may not wonder much about meaning, and will live in pursuit of physical rewards. In time, we may feel isolated, disconnected or depressed because we have no awareness of our Higher Self.

We realign to Divine Light through spiritual practice. Almost any spiritual practice will do—yoga, meditation, journaling, or even spending quiet time by yourself in nature can all serve to reconnect you to your divine origins. One of my favorite practices is to sit quietly for five minutes and gaze into the light of a white candle. This is a simple, but powerful practice. Connecting to a natural light source in this way serves to connect us to our own inner Light.

DIVINE TRUTH

We already discussed some of the essence of Divine Truth earlier in this chapter, when we created our log-on process for beginning our divination sessions. Divine Truth holds the concept of unity. We are all One. Divine

Truth recognizes that we are all on our own individual, unique journey, but are striving for the same happiness, fulfillment and growth. Divine Truth recognizes that we are all equals on this path, and responsible for our own learning. It is the energy of Divine Truth that allows us to intuitively know which path will lead to the fulfillment of our highest path and purpose.

When we are out of alignment with Divine Truth, we may feel the need to persuade others that we are "right," defend our opinions, and judge those that do not agree with our point of view. We start dealing in absolutes, without allowing for other perspectives. Often, this is a mask for insecurity about which path is right for us.

We realign to Divine Truth by letting go of the need to be right. We loosen our grip on what we hold to be true. We embrace the beginner's mind, a state of not knowing anything except that which presents itself in our lives, and open ourselves up to new possibilities of Truth. Truth presents itself most readily when we let go of what we think we know.

DIVINE ABUNDANCE

Divine Abundance allows us to access the infinite resources and responsiveness of our Universe. When we are in alignment with Divine Abundance, we recognize that there is more than enough for everybody. We create out of joyful desire, knowing that we are supported and cared for. We fully expect our desires to manifest themselves into the physical world—and they do.

When we are out of alignment with Abundance, we feel the energies of need and greed at work. We covet what others have, believing that their abundance takes away from ours. We try to hang on to what we have with all our might, afraid of loss.

A wonderful way to realign with Divine Abundance is to give. This acknowledges all of the abundance, all of the resources that you have been blessed with. Through this practice, you will experience that you actually do not miss what you have given away. In fact, you will notice that renewed abundance can flow into your life, now that you have made some room for it.

DIVINE POWER

Divine Power gives us the tremendous gift of free will and free choice. When we align with Divine Power, we recognize that we are creators and are responsible for every aspect of our lives. We know that, no matter what circumstances, the power to make conscious choices always remains with us. We recognize ourselves as the source of our own happiness.

When out of alignment with Divine Power, we feel trapped in our life circumstances. We feel that others have control over us, and that we cannot create change. We blame others for our situations. We may also seek to gain power or control over others to make ourselves feel more secure and powerful.

We realign with Divine Power by taking responsibility for our life circumstances. We acknowledge that we have created our life through our choices, conscious or unconscious. We cultivate an awareness of our available choices as we move forward in our lives, knowing that we have the power to create our experience.

TAKING ACTION

Now is your first opportunity to actually put intuitive information to use! You know in which areas of your life you are out of alignment with your highest path and purpose, and to what degree. You also know which divine universal energy streams are lacking in that life area. And you know how to increase the flow of that particular energy stream. Are you willing to put your new-found knowledge into action?

EXERCISE 3

Choose one of the life areas in which you are out of alignment with your highest path and purpose. Choose three ways in which you can increase the divine universal energy stream that is most lacking in this particular life area within the next week. Create a specific action plan for yourself!

Let's say, for example, that you are 75% aligned with your highest path and purpose in the life area of *"Rest and Relaxation."* You have discovered that the energy most lacking is that of Divine Love. You know, therefore, that this is an area in which you must practice greater self-nurture and self-care. Your action plan may include receiving a massage, setting aside an hour to indulge in a neglected hobby, and taking a bubble bath before bed at least two nights this week.

After following your action plan, dowse again for your alignment with both the divine universal energy stream, and your highest path and purpose. Most likely, both percentages will have shifted towards full alignment.

You may also notice that, as you focus on one life area and increase the flow of one of the divine universal energies, this change will manifest itself in other life areas also. If there were other life areas in which the same energy was lacking, you may wish to dowse again for these alignments, as well.

USING CHARTS

A wonderful tool to use in divination is a chart. Remember how we dowsed for percentages earlier? It was a somewhat tedious process, right? Have a look at the following chart:

PERCENTAGES

	Column A	Column B	Column C	Column D	Column E
Row 1	5	10	15	20	25
Row 2	30	35	40	45	50
Row 3	55	60	65	70	75
Row 4	80	85	90	95	100

Using this chart significantly reduces the number of questions you have to ask to find the right percentage. Here is the line of questioning for this kind of chart:

- *What column contains the correct percentage? Is it in Column A? Is it in Column B? Continue asking for each columns until you receive a "Yes."*

- *Which row contains the correct percentage? Is it in Row 1? Is it in Row 2? Continue asking for each row until you receive a "Yes." This will bring you to the correct answer.*

You can create these charts using all kinds of criteria. Let's say you work with aromatherapy, but aren't sure which essential oils are right for you in a particular situation. You can create this kind of chart containing the names of your different essential oils and simply ask which ones are right for you. Then you can use the percentages chart above to come up with a precise formula for an essential oil remedy!

Similarly, you can create charts with the names of vitamins, Bach flower essences, herbs, healing gemstones, food groups, and so forth. Whenever you find yourself asking for information on a particular subject repeatedly, create a chart and make your divination process more efficient! I've included some additional charts that you can use as templates for creating your own.

AROMATHERAPY OILS

	Column A	Column B	Column C	Column D	Column E
Row 1	Basil	Bergamot	Cedarwood	Chamomile	Clary Sage
Row 2	Coriander	Frankincense	Ginger	Grapefruit	Jasmine
Row 3	Juniper	Lavender	Marjoram	Myrrh	Neroli
Row 4	Patchouli	Peppermint	Rose	Rosemary	Sandalwood

VITAMINS & MINERALS

	Column A	Column B	Column C	Column D	Column E
Row 1	A	Beta Carotene	D	E	K
Row 2	B1 (Thiamine)	B2 (Riboflavin)	B3 (Niacin)	B12	Biotin
Row 3	Folic Acid	C	Calcium	Magnesium	Phosphorus
Row 4	Potassium	Iron	Zinc	Selenium	Manganese

WHEN YOU DO NOT LIKE THE ANSWER

These initial exercises should not yield much controversial information. However, from time to time on your divination journey, you will be tempted to repeat your questions. Usually, you will want to do this when you receive answers that surprise you, make you uncomfortable, or that you simply didn't want to hear. Please resist the temptation of trying to get a different answer if you did not like the first one you received. I generally advise taking the first answer given as the correct one. Do not ask your question over and over again, maybe in slightly different ways. Your Higher Self will eventually consider the question asked and answered. At this point, it will hand the question over to your subconscious, since obviously you were not satisfied with the information that came from your Higher Self. And then you will start getting inconsistent answers, and frustration will set in.

It's fine to ask a question more than once, but after you've asked it twice, you may want to look within yourself and question why you are so dissatisfied with the answer you've received. Is there resistance within you to the information? Was it not what you wanted to hear? Don't start testing or playing games with your Higher Self. If you've followed the process above, your information is accurate and coming from the appropriate source.

Second-guessing the answers usually means that your conscious mind is uncomfortable, and wants to be in charge of the process. Remember that divination initially circumvents the activity of the conscious mind and places it in a position of merely stating the question, and then passively receiving the answer. If your conscious mind loves problem-solving and figuring things out, it may object to this passive role. Our conscious mind loves running the show! Many of us are practically addicted to constant analysis. By second-guessing the information it receives, your conscious mind is merely making its discomfort known. If you find that you are constantly questioning the answers you receive and are often repeating your questions, discipline yourself to take the first answer to your question at face value. You may anticipate a lot of internal resistance to this practice at first. Simply acknowledge the doubts within your conscious mind without investing yourself in them. Observe your mind spin its patterns of doubt, and continue with your dowsing practice. After a while, the doubt mechanisms raised by the conscious mind in order to regain control will subside.

CHAPTER FOUR

POWERFUL QUESTIONS

– THE ART OF ACCESSING INFORMATION

N othing determines the quality of the information you receive more than the quality of the question you ask. When we ask our questions, we need to operate in a way that our Higher Self can understand. We want information from the spiritual plane. Our questioning, therefore, has to align with the frames of reference that are appropriate to the spiritual plane. Remember also that we've asked for all answers to be received in alignment with Divine Truth. This means that the frame of reference we use for our questions must also align with Divine Truth. When you use an inappropriate frame of reference, your Higher Self will allow your subconscious mind to answer the question, and inconsistencies will appear.

Many people who experience frustration with divination because of conflicting and confusing answers are simply not asking the right questions. Save yourself a lot of aggravation and self-doubt by asking appropriately and carefully phrased questions! The specificity of these questions may seem quite tedious at first. However, it serves a very important purpose: to ensure that the intent of your question is crystal clear. The clearer the intent of the question, the clearer and more accurate your answer will be. But let's start first with some common mistakes to avoid!

INEFFECTIVE QUESTIONS

I don't normally like to start a chapter with a negative topic or list of what not to do. However, the way you phrase your questions is so vitally important that I want to start with the types of questions to stay away from in order to receive accurate answers. If you're even remotely thinking of asking the following kinds of questions, *stop!* Keep reading for ways to phrase your questions that will truly yield the quality of information you are looking for.

QUESTIONS CONTAINING THE WORD "SHOULD"

At the top of the list of questions not to ask are any questions containing the word *"should."* As in *"Should I take this job/pursue this relationship/attend this class/etc.?"*

The word *"should"* does not contain any useful frame of reference at all. When my clients ask me if they *"should"* do something, the first thing I ask is *"according to whom?"* The word *"should"* implies an external source of authority and abdicates responsibility. This is why it does not align with Divine Truth. Like it or not, you are 100% in charge of all your own choices. Spirit, your Guides, your Higher Self, all are not responsible for telling you what you *"should"* do. There is a reason that *"should"* is not understood in the spiritual realm. The greatest gift we have is free will and free choice.

Your intuition is designed to serve you as a source of information. Choosing how to act on this information is the prerogative of the conscious mind. So, on a completely practical level, this turn of phrase is not a useful way of accessing information.

The word *"should"* also resonates very strongly on the emotional plane. It is usually generated from a place of confusion, uncertainty, or guilt. The answer to these kinds of questions will come from the information contained within the emotional energy body. Remember that your answers will always align with the frame of reference of the question! The emotional energy body is governed by the subconscious mind, so with the word *"should"* you are actually no longer tapping into the wisdom of your Higher Self at all. Instead, you are receiving information from your subconscious. Keep in mind that, while useful when properly trained, the subconscious is completely unreliable as an accurate source of intuitive information. Most of the time, it tells you what you want to hear. If you ask a question containing the word *"should"* on two different days, chances are that the answers will vary, depending on how you feel at that point in time. Your subconscious will respond based on your emotional state at the time of questioning. This is obviously not the quality of information we want to receive.

Questions containing *"could"* or *"would"* are also rather unproductive. These are usually the words we use when we are trying to avoid the word *"should."* For example: *"Would it serve me to make this choice in order to reach my goal?"* This is definitely a better question than *"Should I do this in order to reach my goal?"* But there is an element of indecision, of ambiguity, in this question. A far better way to phrase this question is *"Is this choice 100% in alignment with my desired outcome?"* This is an incredibly clear question. Note also that this question immediately gives us the opportunity to investigate degrees of alignment through the use of percentages.

The word *"could"* does not align with the frame of reference of the spiritual plane. If you ask *"Could I make this choice in order to reach my goal?"* the answer will usually be *"yes."* This is because, from the perspective of the spiritual plane, we are fully empowered with free will and free choice and can make any choice that we desire.

GOOD, BETTER, BEST

"Good," "better," and *"best"* are very relative terms. It is tempting to ask questions like *"Is it good for me to take this action?"* or *"Is it better for me to make choice A rather than choice B?"* but the problem is that *"good"* and *"better"* are too unspecific. Something could make you feel good or better for the next ten minutes, but not really be in your *"best"* interests in the long term. And what is *"best"* anyway? Equally vague are emotionally descriptive words such as *"practical"* or *"productive"* or even *"fulfilling."* These terms are highly subjective, depending on how we feel while we're asking the question. For example, you might be tempted to ask *"Will it be fulfilling for me to take this job?"* But this question doesn't address a specific level of fulfillment. There is nothing to measure your level of fulfillment against. When we ask questions with an emotional frame of reference, our Higher Self invariably defers to our subconscious for the answer, since it governs our emotions. When you find yourself using these kind of terms, substitute *"my highest path and purpose"* instead. For example *"Is this choice in full alignment with my highest path and purpose?"* is an excellent and very concise question that will yield an accurate answer. I will define this particular frame of reference in greater detail a little later on in this chapter.

WILL I MEET A DARK AND HANDSOME STRANGER?

I am, of course, referring here to questions about the future. The future is, at best, tricky to handle. If asked inappropriately, your Higher Self will once again take information from your subconscious mind—essentially, your opinions, hopes, and desires. Be careful whenever you find yourself asking a question starting with *"Will I ..."* You will get the answer you want to hear! We will discuss appropriate ways to deal with future events and outcomes.

APPROPRIATE FRAMES OF REFERENCE

I'm sure you are realizing that the quality of information you will receive from your Higher Self is highly dependent on the quality of the questions you ask. In order to receive a precise answer, you must establish the appropriate frame of reference. These are frames of reference that are recognized on the spiritual plane. In other words, your Higher Self knows how to operate within these frames of reference, and can give you accurate answers to these types of questions. Below are frames of reference for phrasing your questions in a way that gives you reliable and insightful answers.

1) YOUR HIGHEST PATH AND PURPOSE

Whenever I do research into a client's Soul profile around any particular issue, I use one single frame of reference as my starting point: their Soul's highest path and purpose. Your Soul has chosen to incarnate here in order to grow and evolve. It has chosen specific life lessons to complete for each lifetime. Your Soul came into this lifetime with a plan. Your Soul wants to fully express all its gifts and characteristics into every aspect of your life. This is its highest path and purpose. This is completely understood by your Higher Self. When our life circumstances are in alignment with our Soul's highest path and purpose, we feel a very high level of fulfillment. We also come into alignment with the universal energies of Divine Love, Light, Truth, Abundance, and Power.

Now, this does not mean that there will be no obstacles to overcome on our highest path and purpose. It is, after all, the path that leads to our greatest growth. Sometimes we learn by solving problems and jumping over hurdles. When we tune in to this path, however, we also become very perceptive of our life lessons. We learn and grow more proactively, and we do not need as many negative learning experiences to force us to broaden our perspective.

I would encourage you to use this frame of reference. You no doubt have some specific life situations you want information on. Let's say you are debating a career change. Here are some questions you might wish to ask:

- *Is my current job situation in alignment with my Soul's highest path and purpose?*

- *To what percentage is my current job situation in alignment with my Soul's highest path and purpose? Is it more than 50% aligned? More than 60% aligned?*

(This is an excellent place to put your percentages chart to good use.)

- *Is leaving my company in alignment with my Soul's highest path and purpose?*

- *Is shifting positions within my company in alignment with my Soul's highest path and purpose?*

- *Is a career in Profession A in alignment with my Soul's highest path and purpose?*

- *Is a career in Profession A more in alignment with my Soul's highest path and purpose than Profession B?*

Within this line of questioning, you have the opportunity to get more and more specific about what is most in alignment with your Soul's highest path and purpose. You can research the timing of a career move, the exact direction in which to go, and which combination of the two would work best for you. By finding out the percentage of alignment with your highest path and purpose for the various available options, you can receive incredibly specific information around which choices would lead to the greatest level of fulfillment and growth.

2) A CONSCIOUSLY DESIRED OUTCOME

Never mind our spiritual growth—often, we have a goal of our own in mind! Let's say, for instance, that you are an independent service professional and want to increase your number of new clients by 25%. This is a very specific, consciously desired goal. Here are some questions you might wish to ask:

⬦ *Is my current website content in alignment with my consciously desired goal of increasing my number of new clients by 25%?*

⬦ *Is advertising within this publication in alignment with my consciously desired goal of increasing my number of new clients by 25%?*

⬦ *Is focusing on off-line advertising in alignment with my consciously desired goal of increasing my number of new clients by 25%?*

⬦ *Are my current business practices in alignment with my consciously desired goal of increasing my number of new clients by 25%?*

If you are going to use this kind of frame of reference, it is essential that your goal be as specific as possible. The questions above yield an entirely different quality of information than if the questions were stated:

⬦ *Is my current website content in alignment with my consciously desired goal of increasing my number of new clients?*

This kind of broader line of questioning will give you answers that, while still accurate, reflect the lack of specific intent behind the inquiry. Sometimes, of course, you may not have a very specific desired outcome, and then it is perfectly appropriate to word your questions within a broader frame of reference.

A very important question that is always worth asking when it comes to any consciously desired goal or outcome is:

⬦ *Is this consciously desired goal in alignment with my Soul's highest path and purpose?*

Asking this question is a wonderful way of checking that what you desire is also what your Higher Self desires for you! When the two are at odds, your Higher Self will only participate in the manifestation of your goal on the physical plane in a limited way. In order to truly harness your spiritual resources when it comes to manifesting the outcomes you desire, your Higher Self needs to be completely on board. This means that you will have a much easier time reaching those goals that also align with your Soul's highest path and purpose. If your consciously desired goal and your highest path and purpose do not align, you might want to ask:

> ❖ *To what percentage does my consciously desired goal align with my Soul's highest path and purpose? Is it more than 50%? More than 60%? Etc.*

You will often find that you are only away from full alignment by a few percentage points. You may want to "tweak" some elements of your goal, such as your timeline, in order to bring your goal into full alignment with your highest path and purpose. This will assist you in manifesting your goals with far greater ease and speed, because you have the resources of your Higher Self working with you.

3) A LIFE LESSON

Sometimes we struggle to understand why we are in certain situations. Especially in times of hardship, it is often difficult to see patterns and design within our life experiences. If you are struggling to gain understanding, in good situations or in bad, you may wish to use a life lesson as a frame of reference. Our life lessons offer us both positive and negative learning experiences. Essentially, we can learn from positive events taking place in our lives, or we can learn by overcoming obstacles and hardship. Here are some questions you might wish to ask:

> ❖ *Is my current experience of… an expression of a life lesson my Soul chose before incarnation?*

> ❖ *Is my other current experience of… an expression of the same life lesson?*

◆ *Were my past experiences of ... and ... an expression of the same life lesson?*

◆ *To what percentage have I completed this life lesson?*

◆ *Was the past experience of ... a positive learning experience within this life lesson?*

◆ *Is my present experience of ... a negative learning experience within this life lesson?*

◆ *Was my experience with person ... part of my own life lesson, that person's life lesson, or both of ours?*

◆ *Do I have a Soul-level agreement with this person to assist me in completing a life lesson? Is it through a positive learning experience within this life lesson? Is it through a negative learning experience within this life lesson?*

Through this kind of questioning, you can begin to tie the various events in your life together and start seeing the patterns and design within your experiences and relationships. If you start to recognize what the particular life lesson is about, you may even wish to ask:

◆ *Does this particular life lesson center around the subject of ...?*

3ʀᴅ DIMENSIONAL FRAMES OF REFERENCE

Your Higher Self and your Spirit Guides don't actually hang about and observe you in everyday life. They are not little flies on the wall. Unless you have been fully connected with your Higher Self in the past (and you might want to do some divination to find out how connected you were to your Higher Self before you completed the connection process in Chapter Two), it has been gathering information about your current circumstances from your subtle energy bodies. If you've not been communicating consciously very much with your Higher Self until now, it may not really be familiar with some of the concepts we use in everyday life.

Your Higher Self may not, for instance, be familiar with the concept of money. Money is the way we exchange energy here. It is not a concept in the spiritual realm. Similarly, your Higher Self may not understand 3rd dimensionally-based concepts like a job, divorce, alimony, credit cards, banks, or even ownership of physical property. Essentially, if it does not exist in the spiritual realm, and you haven't been communicating with your Higher Self about it, it may have no idea what you are asking about.

Just to be sure, you may want to create a line of questioning such as:

♦ *Is the concept of money such as we use it within our physical dimension, as well as my personal financial situation, within my Higher Self's current frame of reference?*

If the answer is *"no,"* you might want to take the time to explain it to your Higher Self, and then repeat the question to make sure that the concept is now clear. I know this sounds odd—after all, your Higher Self is all-knowing. But remember that its all-knowingness is confined to the spiritual plane. In this case, you might want to say something like: *"Money or currency is what we exchange for goods and services here in the third dimension. I currently make [insert amount] every month, which I use to pay for my home, the food my body needs, this book, and any other objects I acquire. I receive money from my employer for the services I provide him, and in turn, I exchange that money to provide for myself everything else I need or want here in the physical plane. I'd like to increase my overall income by [insert amount] monthly, in alignment with my highest path and purpose."*

If you've been 100% connected to your Higher Self for a while, it may not need to brush up on these 3rd dimensional concepts. You've been in communication long enough that it is probably familiar with these matters.

Likewise, once your Higher Self has included a concept into its frame of reference, there is no need to repeat it. But at the start of your divination journey, it can lead to great confusion if you are asking questions about your job, and your Higher Self has no clear concept of what a "job" is.

LINEAR TIME

Again, remember that your Higher Self exists on the spiritual plane, which is located outside of linear time as we know it. Linear time is an organizational construct that exists here in the third dimension for the sake of our growth and learning through the consequences of our choices and actions. This kind of growth could not take place were it not for the sequential nature of our lives.

Your Higher Self, however, may need you to include the phrase *"in linear time"* in any questions that include a mention of time frames.

QUESTIONS ABOUT THE FUTURE

We just can't seem to help ourselves—peeking at future events and accurately predicting future outcomes remains a fascinating endeavor. I am fairly sure you will want to question your Higher Self about what may lie in store for you along your path. However, there are some guidelines you must keep in mind when asking questions about the future.

The future is constantly shifting and changing. It is an evolving, malleable composite of probable and possible outcomes. In other words, nothing is certain. The future depends on all the choices you make today, and all the choices everyone you interact with also makes.

Let's say you decide to sit down at your favorite coffee shop to read the paper, instead of having your coffee on the go, the way you normally do. Five minutes later, your high school sweetheart walks in. You reconnect and start dating again. Maybe you even get married!

Now, let's say you decide not to dawdle and have your coffee on the go, even though you really would like to read the paper. But you forgot last night to iron your shirt, so now you are running late because you had to do it this morning. You leave the coffee shop, and your high school sweetheart walks in right after you leave. You don't reconnect.

These are two different scenarios based entirely on one choice. What if the sweetheart also decides to just have coffee at the office? What if it rains that day and neither of you wants to get out of the car in the rain just for a cup of coffee?

There are so many variables to the future! Of course, if the two people in the above scenario have a Soul-level agreement to connect in this lifetime, eventually they will create the events that will bring them together. But that may be next week, or next year, or even five years from now.

First of all, when you ask questions about future events, you must recognize that all answers come from the perspective of the present moment. Your Higher Self will give you the answer based on circumstances as they are right now. It receives input from your current frame of mind, your emotional state, and present inclinations towards one choice or another. In other words, depending whether you're in an optimistic, motivated state of mind, or a depressed, hopeless mood, answers about the future may conflict from one day to the next.

Also, you may want to consider how much you really want to know about your future. Are you merely curious? Or are you looking for accurate guidance in pursuit of a personal goal? Ask yourself, before you proceed, how disappointing or unexpected answers might affect your future outlook. The future is sometimes hidden from us for a good reason.

So how do we ask questions regarding future events? When we deal with the future, we formulate our questions based on current possibility and probability. Rather than asking, *"Will I receive a promotion?"* we ask:

◈ *Is there a probability of receiving a promotion?* If no, continue with:

◈ *Is there a possibility of receiving a promotion?*

If yes to either of these, ask:

◈ *To what percentage is receiving a promotion possible/probable?*

All possibilities and probabilities can be measured in percentages. This is an incredibly useful tool in gaining information about the future. After all, there is a big difference between something being 12% probable, and 85% probable! You can now further refine your questioning to include specific time frames.

◈ *To what percentage is it possible/probable that I will receive a promotion within six months?*

◈ *To what percentage is it possible/probable that I will receive a promotion within one year?*

You will most likely find that the percentages shift as you explore the different time fames. This is a very precise way of gaining information around the future. Remember, however, that all information is given from the perspective of the present moment. All the choices you make today can have an effect on the probabilities of future outcomes. For example, if you choose to hand a report in late or miss a meeting, it may affect the probability of your receiving a promotion.

We live our lives journeying from one "choice point" to the next. "Choice points" are what I call those moments in life where we have to make decisions that will potentially affect us in the future. They are not the small day-to-day decisions about what to have for lunch. They are decisions about the direction of your business, or which job offer to pursue, or whether to break up with your girlfriend. When we arrive at a choice point in life, we tend to feel as if we've stopped moving. We are in a position of plotting our next course. This is usually when we most need guidance around the future.

Sometimes we get stuck at these choice points, unwilling to make a decision. For example, three or four different business opportunities may present themselves all at once, and you are left wondering which is most appropriate for your business. It can be tremendously helpful to receive information about what awaits us along one particular road or another, to assist us in moving forward in alignment with our highest path and purpose.

When we come to a choice point, there are usually five possible paths available to us. When we are traveling along one of these pathways, we have a sense of going somewhere. We are in the middle of a joint business venture or have decided to pursue a specific opportunity, and the consequences of that choice are now playing themselves out. Our course, at least for the foreseeable future (which could be the next two weeks or two months) is set. I call these paths "energetic pathways of possibility." They are the likely directions available to us, based on where we are in our lives right now. Now, some of these paths will be more probable—and more in alignment with our highest path and purpose—than others.

So, let's talk about how to use this information to structure productive questions that will yield accurate answers. Let's say you've arrived at a choice point in your business. You want to take your business to a new level, but aren't sure of how to go about it. All you know is that something needs to change in order for growth to occur. What you do know is the amount of income you'd like to expand into.

To begin with, clearly state your consciously desired outcome to your Higher Self. In this case, your consciously desired outcome would be to expand your business to create a certain amount in revenue monthly. Your line of questioning can then be:

◊ *Is there a current pathway of possibility available to me at this time that connects me to my consciously desired outcome?*

What you are asking here is if there is an available path at this point in time that leads to your goal. This is an energetic connection, if you will, to your desired outcome. Let's say the answer here is *"no."* Don't give up yet! Here are some more questions with which to pursue information.

◈ *Is there a pathway of possibility that will become available to me within the next (month, two months, etc.) that connects me to my consciously desired outcome?*

◈ *Is there a current choice before me that will make this pathway of possibility more probable to manifest itself in my life?*

◈ *Is there an action I can take right now that will create a pathway of possibility towards my consciously desired outcome?*

◈ *Is there a choice that will likely be before me in [insert time frame] that will create a pathway of possibility towards my consciously desired outcome?*

◈ *From the perspective of the present moment, at which point in linear time is a pathway of possibility likely to become available to me? In one month? Six months? A year?*

Now, if the first four questions in the above paragraph all were answered with a resounding *"no,"* you may as well ask:

◈ *Is there a possibility of this consciously desired outcome manifesting itself at any time in my life, from the perspective of the present moment?*

◈ *Are there any actions or choices available to me that will create the possibility of this consciously desired outcome manifesting itself at any time in my life?*

Most of the time, our desired outcomes are available to us. We don't conceive of them otherwise. The above questions will give you an idea how far away from your desired outcome you are. You may be nowhere near it, or it may be right around the corner. Maybe your business does not align with your highest path and purpose at all, and expansion is highly unlikely because the entire business simply does not serve you. But if an energetic connection, a path of possibility exists, then you can travel along that energy of possibility to make your goal more and more probable, the closer you get.

Now, occasionally, people do conceive of goals that are so far away from their path and purpose that absolutely no chance exists. I'm thinking of some of those people who audition for *"American Idol"* without ever having sung before in their lives! People who aspire to highly improbable goals usually have some severe energetic blocks and restrictions in their record that are not allowing them to access information appropriate to their lifetime's path. While rare, it does happen. So, if you get a *"no"* on those last two questions, you may want to have another look at your desired outcome. Pursuing your goal may end up feeling like you are banging your head against an invisible wall. This line of questioning can save you a lot of time and energy.

For the most part, though, you will discover that a path of possibility is either available to you right now, or will arise some time in the foreseeable future, based on your present situation.

Now, let's go back to our original question:

◈ *Is there a current pathway of possibility available to me at this time that connects me to my consciously desired outcome?*

If you receive a *"yes,"* you know that, based on your current life situation, your consciously desired outcome is a possibility. So let's continue this line of questioning.

◈ *From the perspective of the present moment, how probable is the manifestation of my consciously desired outcome? Is it 50% probable? 60% probable? 100% probable?*

◈ *From the perspective of the present moment, how probable is the manifestation of my consciously desired outcome within six months? A year?*

◆ *Are there possible pathways I can choose/actions I can take right now that will make the manifestation of my consciously desired outcome more probable?*

Let's say that the answer to this last question was a resounding *"yes."* Upon introspection, the five available pathways of possibility become clearer to you. These will all have been possibilities that, to one degree or another, have been flitting around in your mind as you ponder your next move. You could, at this point in time:

A. Do nothing and keep your business exactly as it is. This avenue is always a possibility—to stay exactly where you are.

B. To take on an active business partner.

C. To pursue training in a new direction that you could add to your existing offerings.

D. To diversify and expand your market.

E. To develop a new product specifically geared towards your current customers.

You could then ask the following questions to determine the course of action most likely to create the business expansion you desire.

◆ *Which pathway of possibility most aligns with my desired outcome of expanding my business to create $$$ in revenue monthly? Is it pathway A? Is it pathway B? Etc.?*

For each pathway listed above, you can also ask:

◆ *If I make this choice, is the manifestation of my consciously desired outcome more probable? Less probable? To what percentage probable?*

◈ *Does this choice influence the time frame within which my consciously desired outcome is likely to manifest? By how many months/weeks/years? In linear time, does my consciously desired outcome move closer to me when I make this choice? Or further away?*

Remember that all of the answers you receive will come from the perspective of your current life circumstances. In one month, or two months, you may receive different answers. However, with this kind of questioning, you can receive a very accurate and consistent picture of the future. When you repeat these kinds of questions after a month or so, you may find that percentages of probability or possibility have fluctuated, or that time frames have shifted. This can then tell you whether you have been pursuing your desired outcome effectively. By using percentages of probability and possibility, your Higher Self has a way to express the likelihood of future outcomes in a way that aligns with Divine Truth.

Once again, please do not repeat these kinds of questions on a daily basis. If you feel the need to do so, you are probably not willing to receive the answers your Higher Self has to offer. You can check in to any current life situation every month or so, or more often if there have been a lot of changes going on in your life that may affect that particular situation.

Lastly, if you are receiving a lot of *"maybe"* answers or there seems to be some reluctance in the quality of the answers you are receiving, you may ask the following:

◈ *Is it appropriate at this time for me to gather information about this consciously desired outcome?*

Sometimes, knowledge about your future is not appropriate for you to have right now. Sometimes it might affect how you absolve your life lessons, or may negatively influence your choices. With this question, allow your Higher Self to guide you towards what is appropriate for you to know. If you receive a negative response and are really disappointed, you might even want to ask:

♦ *Will it be appropriate for me to gather information about this consciously desired outcome in one month? Two weeks? Etc.*

That way, you know that your Higher Self is merely asking you to hold off for a short time. Simply put off this line of questioning until it is in alignment with your highest path and purpose to receive the information you desire.

QUESTIONS ABOUT OTHER PEOPLE

Let me be clear: your Higher Self has no access to Soul-level information for others, unless these other people have a direct and meaningful impact on you. But even in this case, your Higher Self knows only your perspective within the interaction.

In order to "log on" to someone else's Higher Self and spiritual-level information, you must access their Akashic Record. This is a far more advanced topic outside of the scope of this book. If you are interested in conducting intuitive readings on behalf of others, I offer a professional intuitive training course on my website. Please do not use the techniques outlined in this book to give others information about themselves. What you may end up receiving is information contained within their subtle energy bodies. However, this information will not come from their Higher Self, and it will not have the same accuracy or reliability. It can be very damaging for people to receive inaccurate information from an intuitive source. Unless you are thoroughly trained by an experienced and credible intuitive professional, you should not offer intuitive insight that could have an impact on other people's lives.

It is also inappropriate to use your intuition to try and pry into the lives of others to satisfy your own curiosity. If you are wondering whether your best friend's boyfriend will propose to her, do not pick up your pendulum! It's none of your business, and your Higher Self does not have access to that information, anyway.

Now, if you are wondering whether your own boyfriend will propose (or your girlfriend will say *"yes"*), that's a different story. But instead of asking, *"Will my boyfriend propose to me within one month?"* the more appropriate line of questioning would be:

◆ *From the perspective of the present moment, is it probable that I will receive a proposal from my boyfriend within one month? To what percentage is it probable?*

This way, the question is about you, not your boyfriend. While you're asking about this life situation, you may want to ensure that your Higher Self understands the 3rd dimensional concepts of "proposals" and "engagement"—and, for that matter, the concept of "marriage."

QUESTIONS ABOUT RELATIONSHIPS

Relationships are an important and essential part of our lives, our growth and our personal and spiritual development. We are here to assist each other in growing and learning. We can draw on the wealth of someone else's experiences so we do not have to learn the same lessons in our own lives. We are here to support, assist and sometimes challenge each other towards our next level of consciousness.

Let's start with the topic on which I probably receive the most questions—Soulmates.

ABOUT SOULMATES

People are fascinated by the idea of a Soulmate. It seems like such a romantic idea—one person who is our ideal mate, destined for us in this lifetime.

Unfortunately, the reality of the Soulmate isn't so romantic. Some people do indeed have a Soulmate contract with another Soul. This situation isn't always in alignment with either person's highest path and purpose. Contracts are binding, lifetime after lifetime after lifetime, unless we specifically ask for them to be removed from our Soul record. Contracts were a tool that for a while served us in learning our life lessons. Essentially, they ensured that we would do our spiritual development work with each other, even when it would have been easier not to. However, we have evolved beyond the need for contracts. Some Souls, though, have kept contracts current in their record.

Two Souls who are contracted as Soulmates will meet, over and over again, lifetime after lifetime, regardless of whether they are still learning from each other or not. They may stay locked in unjustified karma, working on long-absolved life lessons time after time in a frustrating, pointless dance. Sometimes, of course, these relationships can be beneficial. Certainly, in the lifetime of the contract's origin, these two Souls created such a strong bond that they promised each other to do spiritual development work together in all subsequent lifetimes. However, Souls do grow and develop in different directions—just like people themselves do.

What is far more beneficial to the growth and evolution of our Souls is a Soul-level agreement to do spiritual development work together. These agreements are made together before incarnating, for a specific lifetime. They are not a permanent fixture in our Soul record. Of course, many Souls choose to work together many lifetimes in a row. That is a very beautiful thing, when it is mutually beneficial for each Soul's growth and learning. We all have many Souls in our lives—family, friends, spouses, and lovers— that we've met before.

So, in my experience, Soulmates aren't really all they are reputed to be. Neither bad nor good, they are a contract between two Souls that may or may not serve them. Soul-level agreements are better.

If there is a Soul-level agreement between two Souls, events will transpire to bring them together in their life's journey if and when it is appropriate. Our Higher Selves see to it that, when we are ready, our partner in learning will appear. We don't need to go chasing after them—they will present themselves with perfect, divine timing. If you are wondering if you and your partner were "meant to be," a more appropriate line of questioning is:

⬧ *Do this person and I have a Soul-level agreement to complete spiritual development work together within this lifetime?*

⬧ *Is this spiritual development work still in alignment with my highest path and purpose?*

⬧ *Do this person and I have an agreement to do this spiritual development work within a romantic, long-term, intimate relationship?*

⬧ *Do this person and I have an agreement to do our spiritual development work together through finding fulfillment within a romantic, long-term, intimate relationship?*

⬧ *Do this person and I have an agreement to do our spiritual development work together through finding challenges within a romantic, long-term, intimate relationship?*

⬧ *Does our agreement include the 3rd dimensional concept of marriage?*

⬧ *Does our agreement include having children together?*

⬧ *Is a romantic, long-term, intimate relationship with this person in alignment with my Soul's highest path and purpose?*

⬧ *Is a friendship with this person in alignment with my Soul's highest path and purpose?*

Once again, your Higher Self may not consider it appropriate for you to have answers to these questions right now. If conflicting answers present themselves, please ask whether this line of questioning is available to you at this time.

Please also note my terminology of a *"romantic, long-term, intimate relationship,"* rather than using labels such as "marriage." Our concept of marriage is a 3rd dimensional one and is not used in the spiritual realm. At the spiritual level, the purpose of relationships is to support each other's growth and development towards a new level of consciousness. Legally binding promises of being together for the remainder of this lifetime are considered unimportant. If you are using the concept of "marriage" in any of your questions, please ensure that your Higher Self understands this frame of reference.

Have a look at the second question on this list. Sometimes we have a Soul-level agreement with someone—but it is around a lesson that we have already completed in another way. Remember that we are presented with many, many opportunities to grow and learn our lessons in our lifetime. It may well be that a person presents him or herself in your life, and though you are drawn to each other because of the agreement, you actually have no further need for the work that your two Souls agreed to do together. In that case, the relationship, while it may be a pleasant one, would not contribute to your spiritual growth.

Notice the question: *"Do this person and I have an agreement to do our spiritual development work together through finding fulfillment within a romantic, long-term, intimate relationship?"* As this question implies, having an agreement to complete spiritual development work together— or even a relationship being in alignment with your Soul's highest path and purpose—does not necessarily imply a "happily ever after." It is even possible for us to have a one-sided romantic relationship that we learn from—and our agreement with the other person is that they present us with the opportunity to experience unrequited love, for example. This relationship, though unhappy, may then still align with your highest path and purpose.

You may, for instance, ask:

- *Is the Soul-level agreement to do spiritual development work together with this person based on positive learning experiences? Or negative learning experiences?*

And, if the answer here is *"negative learning experiences:"*

- *Is it in alignment with my highest path and purpose to enter into a relationship with this person at this time? What kind of relationship would be most in alignment with my highest path and purpose? A romantic one? A friendship? Etc.?*

You see, the nature of the relationship may not be detailed in your Soul-level agreement. You may have an agreement that includes negative learning experiences, for instance, in which the other person betrays your trust. However, whether this takes place within a romantic relationship, a friendship, or a social acquaintance, is not specified. In this case, the learning experience of having your trust betrayed can have very little impact on your life (if you maintain a relationship of social acquaintance) or an enormous impact on your life (if you were to marry this person.) Either way, you can complete your agreement and learn your life lesson. Now, if it is truly in your highest path and purpose to have a negative learning experience around betrayal, and marriage is part of the Soul-level agreement, then I doubt you would receive information from your Higher Self around this. However, in my experience, our Higher Self happily works with us to minimize the negative impact certain learning experiences might have on our lives. We are not here to be miserable!

By finding out the details of our Soul-level agreements, we can be spared a great deal of time and energy that we might invest in unproductive relationships that do not lead to growth or fulfillment.

Only rarely do you not have a Soul-level agreement with the people you attract into your life. Usually, you will be drawn to Souls that you have an agreement with. From time to time, however, it may happen that you are in a relationship where no Soul-level agreement exists. Again, the main question here is:

⬧ *Is a relationship (specify the type of relationship!) with this person in alignment with my Soul's highest Path and Purpose?*

You may wish to pursue a relationship, even if the answer here is *"no."* Remember, though, that we tend to thrive and feel a great deal of fulfillment when we align with our highest path and purpose. That is, after all, what we are here for.

NEXT STEPS

Now that we've covered some of these guidelines, you probably realize that a lot of thought goes into the appropriate phrasing of the questions in divination. Remember that the quality of the questions you ask directly determines the quality of the information you receive.

If you are not sure if your question's frame of reference aligns with Divine Truth, simply ask!

⬧ *Does the question "..." allow for accurate answers to come from my Higher Self, in alignment with Divine Truth?*

Let your Higher Self teach you how to appropriately phrase your questions. It may take some practice for appropriate questioning, in alignment with Divine Truth, to become second-nature. However, this is a crucial skill to develop. Our questions allow us to access a wealth of information—but that information is only as useful and accurate as our questioning allows. Asking appropriately formulated *"yes"* and *"no"* questions now will serve us well later on in this book, when we expand our lines of questioning to open-ended questions. Then, even more than now, it will be crucial that our questions align with Divine Truth.

Before you move on to the next chapter of this book, it is important for you develop a high level of comfort with these *"yes"* and *"no"* questions.

EXERCISE

For the next two weeks, ask your Higher Self at least twenty questions every day, using *"yes"* and *"no"* questions that align with Divine Truth. Keep a journal of the questions you ask, and the corresponding answers you receive. Journaling pages are included in the free workbook, which you may download at http://www.EmpoweredSoul.com/workbook.htm

I know that this exercise may seem like a lot of time spent, and a lot of questions asked, however, laying a solid foundation in divination will give you confidence as we progress through the next chapters of this book. You will become more creative with your questions after a week or so— and receive lots of useful information! You will have plenty of practice in phrasing your own questions in alignment with Divine Truth.

Remember to start each round of divination with the same *"log on"* process that we created in Chapter 3. It is important that you remain consistent. Don't skip this step, or you will have no way of knowing that your answers are coming from the intended source. Diligence now will pay off down the road!

By asking this many questions of your Higher Self, you will find yourself applying your intuition to more and more areas of your life. By going through such an extensive process of questioning, you will have to stretch your imagination to find new things to ask your Higher Self about. You will realize in how many different ways your intuition can serve you. You will get a sense of just how broadly and extensively your new skills can be applied, and what a wealth of information is available to you.

If you are concerned about running out of questions for your Higher Self, I encourage you to ask questions regarding the choices that you already make every single day. Take a look at the various life areas that we have already worked with—Profession, Finance, Physical Well-Being, Intimate Relationships, Friendships, Family, Personal Development, Spiritual Development, Physical

Surroundings, and Rest and Relaxation. What choices are available to you in these life areas today, tomorrow, or throughout this week?

Take the life area of your physical well-being, for example. If you have a regular exercise routine, you might want to explore whether it still serves your desired outcome. You may want to work with your Higher Self on what other physical activities may align with your highest path and purpose right now. You can also ask questions around your diet. Are you making food choices in full alignment with your highest path and purpose? What foods would serve you towards greater health and well-being right now? This information can change daily!

Consider using your intuition to make the most out of your professional life. If your "to-do" list is overloaded, you can ask which projects are most in alignment with your highest path and purpose to tackle right now. You can work with your Higher Self on structuring your calendar in a way that reduces your stress level. You can find out which relationships at work serve your highest path and purpose.

You can also determine intuitively what activities would serve your highest path and purpose in your personal time. Perhaps there are undiscovered or neglected hobbies that you might wish to ask about. If you have a choice of movies to see this weekend, ask your Higher Self which movie would most serve your highest path and purpose!

This practice will dramatically shift your level of consciousness. By applying your intuition to the many mundane choices you make every day, you will recognize how your decisions determine the quality of your life experiences. You will also realize just how many choices you have been making unconsciously! There are no insignificant or irrelevant questions in this process. Every choice you make has the potential to be life-changing. When your everyday choices align with your highest path and purpose, your level of contentment and satisfaction will increase. Through this practice, you can achieve a very high level of fulfillment in your life.

GAINING CONFIDENCE

When we first start working with our intuition, we have a great investment in being right. We crave validation of our own accuracy. This system of intuitive access is designed to deliver information with a very high degree of accuracy. However, the only real way that you will ever build confidence and trust in the information you are receiving is to take the leap and act on that information. Base some of your every day actions on the information received from your Higher Self. Then notice how things unfold. Remember that intuitive information does not create upheaval. It guides us and assists us, one choice at a time.

Start acting on the information your Higher Self gives you. Notice the consequences of these actions. This is why keeping a journal is so important. As you start living through intuitive guidance, and begin recognizing the positive consequences of doing so, you will begin to trust your intuition more and more. Consequently, you will put the information to use more often, with more confidence, which in turn will lead to more excellent results in your life. Your confidence in your intuitive abilities will then grow. Start with small leaps of faith. There is no substitute for the experience of living according to your intuition and seeing the results in your own life. Within a few months, you will gain unshakeable confidence in the information received from your Higher Self. A few months may sound like a long time to gain faith and trust in your intuition, but remember that your intuitive abilities will serve you for the rest of your life.

Keep in mind that you remain responsible for the consequences of your choices and actions at all times. Using your intuition to access additional information about your available choices in no way means abdicating responsibility for those choices.

CHAPTER FIVE

INTERNALIZING THE INTUITIVE PROCESS

B y now, you have no doubt realized what a vast amount of information you can access through carefully worded *"yes"* and *"no"* questions. Over the past two weeks, you've become truly comfortable with your method of divination, and have likely learned a great deal about yourself. You have gained a new perspective about just how useful your intuition can be in providing information to you about many, many different areas of your life. Phrasing questions appropriately in alignment with Divine Truth probably feels like second-nature to you by now. This will remain an essential skill as we expand from *"yes"* and *"no"* questions to open-ended questions, which is, of course, what we are really after. We wish to access a flow of information when we open ourselves up with a question. We want to communicate with our Higher Selves as if we were sitting down with a knowledgeable friend over a cup of coffee. Remember, our methods of divination were just a place to start.

If you chose to continue asking only *"yes"* or *"no"* questions and proceeded no further through this book, you would already have an incredible amount of intuitive information available to you. With *"yes"* or *"no"* questions, though, you are limited to your own frames of reference. You can only ask questions about what is already known to you. With open-ended lines of questioning, however, our Higher Self can teach us new frames of reference. We can receive answers that include previously unknown concepts and possibilities. As we expand our horizons to include open-ended questions, we will frequently return to the clarity and simplicity of *"yes"* and *"no."* So don't put that pendulum away just yet!

Hopefully, you have completed all of the exercises outlined in this book so far and have diligently asked your Higher Self numerous questions over the past two weeks. These next chapters are based on the assumption that you have developed a solid foundation and high level of comfort with your method of divination.

Chances are that over the past few weeks, you've been staring at your pendulum with rapt attention, watching it swing seemingly of its own accord. Perhaps you've been working really hard to keep the fingers of your hand rigid while muscle-testing, only to find that the method works anyway! Remember that these are just external indicators of the answers that you are receiving internally.

Some of your conscious skepticism about divination has most likely been put to rest. You've probably noticed that the answers you've received so far weren't all that surprising. Maybe they just affirmed what you already knew in the back of your head, or in your heart. This is a very good thing. Remember that your intuition has always been a part of you. The information you are now accessing through divination has been available to you all along. You've probably by now developed some faith in the answers you're receiving. It is essential that some of the doubts within your conscious mind have been put to rest before moving on to the next step.

Your subconscious has been giving your body the signals that make your pendulum swing, or that make your fingers stay rigid or go weak. So far, the subconscious has been receiving messages from your Higher Self, and has been relaying them to you via the pendulum, or muscle testing. As you've asked more and more questions over the past few weeks, you may have noticed that you had a good idea of the answer before you even dowsed or muscle-tested. You may have realized that there are subtle, internal signals for *"yes"* or *"no"* that have nothing to do with your subconscious mind creating the movements of the pendulum or the rigidity of your fingers.

Consciously tuning in to the internal perception of the answers we receive through divination will be the focus as we continue through this book. So far, we've excluded the conscious mind from receiving answers and have relegated it to a passive role of observer. We've let our subconscious be in charge of receiving information from our Higher Self and translating these into our method of divination. We are now going to allow our conscious mind to take a slightly more active part of the process.

DEVELOPING INNER AWARENESS

Our next step is to cultivate awareness of the inner aspect of intuitive information. We can learn to perceive the answers from our Higher Self internally, without relying on divination. Our Higher Self communicates with us through small and subtle signals that vary for each person. Everyone will have their very own unique internal receptors for intuitive information. The process will be different for every single person reading this book. The next chapters will assist you in tuning in to your own personal way of receiving intuitive information. This is a very highly individual process. Just as people communicate differently with each other, you and your Higher

Self will have your own unique style of interaction. You probably have never consciously explored this communication style.

As you dowse or muscle test, notice how the answers resonate inside of yourself. This internal perception of the answers can take lots of different forms. Notice whether you see a *"yes"* or *"no"* flash in your mind's eye. You may see a red light for *"no,"* and a green light for *"yes."* Perhaps you hear the words *"yes"* or *"no"* inside your head. Perhaps you feel a sense of rightness in the pit of your stomach. Perhaps it's a combination of the above cues. These signals may at first be so subtle that they are barely perceptible.

EXERCISE

Ask ten questions of your Higher Self. Pay close attention to what is happening inside of you. Write a detailed description of what you feel, see, hear, or if words pop into your head. Don't worry at this time if you think you're just imagining things. Write down your internal experience of divination.

Please note that the conscious mind is now playing the role of both the questioner, and as the conscious and alert receiver of the answers. At first, the internal aspects of the answers may be frustratingly subtle. Give yourself some time with this. As you practice, they will become more and more obvious. Eventually, they will become a familiar, completely distinct energy resonating within you. This is a process that cannot be rushed. It takes mindful observation of what is going on in your mind and in your body while you dowse or muscle test.

EXERCISE

Instead of asking your questions with pendulum in hand, or with fingers interlocked for muscle testing, close your eyes first. Take a breath and focus on how you feel inside. Focus your vision into the darkness behind your eyes. Then ask your question. Even if you receive no internal signals whatsoever, take your best guess as to whether the answer was *"yes"* or *"no."* Then dowse or muscle test to confirm the answer. Note how often your guess was correct.

LET YOUR IMAGINATION BE YOUR GUIDE

The following exercises will help you further tune in to the internal aspects of your divination process.

EXERCISE

Grab a piece of paper and pencil and have them ready. Read through the following brief paragraph, then close your eyes and let your imagination take flight.

Imagine yourself in a beautiful place. You are sitting in the warm sun, and the temperature is just right. There is a light breeze. You are near water. You may be on a beach, or by a pool, or in a meadow by a stream. You are drinking something. You might be sipping iced tea, or a drink with a little umbrella in it. Perhaps you are alone, or in good company. Take a little vacation for a full sixty seconds by closing your eyes right now. When you are finished, open your eyes and read on.

Now answer the following questions. There are no right answers in this exercise. Please simply mark which questions were most easily answered. Do not think too much about the answer. If you cannot immediately answer a question, move on to the next.

Did you feel the warm sun on your body?
Did you taste the drink in your mouth?
Could you feel a cold glass in your hand?

Can you describe your surroundings in detail?
What did your drink look like?
How did the sunlight look, reflecting off the water?

Were you narrating your scene in your head?
Were you having a conversation with someone?
As you remember your scene, do descriptive words come to mind?

Could you hear the sound of the water?
Was there any background noise going on?
Could you hear the breeze in the trees?

How easily you answered these questions can give you clues as to what you're looking for internally when you are dowsing.

If you answered the first set of questions most easily, you may wish to investigate how a *"yes"* or *"no"* feels internally. Your answers may be accompanied by a physical sensation. Or you might receive an emotional feeling of rightness or wrongness. Your intuition may come most easily to you on a kinesthetic level.

If you answered the second set of questions most easily, you may have a difficult time not staring at your hands or pendulum! Close your eyes during divination and investigate whether there is a visual representation of the answer in your mind's eye. You may see the words *"yes"* or *"no"* flash before you. The answers may also be associated with a particular color, such as red for *"no"* and green for *"yes."* Your intuition may come most easily to you on a visual level.

If you answered the third set of questions most easily, you may want to look for the words *"yes"* and *"no"* to pop into your head. This will not necessarily be an auditory phenomenon. You'll simply receive the word into your mind. You may find yourself internally speaking along with your pendulum. Your intuition may come most easily to you on a verbal level.

If you answered the fourth set of questions most easily, you may wish to investigate what you hear internally when you are dowsing. You may perhaps hear the words *"yes"* or *"no"* inside your head. The words may be pitched inside your head in a particular way. Perhaps the internal voice you hear has a particular quality or sound to it. Your intuition may come most easily to you on an auditory level.

What if you answered more than one set of questions with ease? Then look for internal answers that carry both qualities.

EXERCISE

Ask 10 more questions of your Higher Self. Using the information gained from the exercise above, pay close attention to what is happening inside of you. Once again, write a detailed description of what you feel, see, hear, or if words pop into your head.

With a little bit of practice and mindful awareness, you will begin to tune in to the answers you are receiving internally, even before you divine the answers. When you become more experienced at this, you will start to rely primarily on your internal messages. Dowsing and muscle testing will merely serve as confirmation of your internal intuitive awareness.

IMAGINATION OR INTUITION?

By now you're probably wondering why we want to use our imagination in this process at all. *"How do I know it's really my intuition talking? How do I know I'm not just making things up?"* This is one of the biggest concerns many people have when it comes to accessing their intuition.

Our intuition is always "on." It is constantly giving us information, every day of our lives. Imagine a radio music station, running quietly in the background, wherever you are, whatever you may be doing. The music is so omnipresent that you don't even really hear it anymore. Every once in a while you may catch an auditory glimpse of it, a sweet chord that all too soon gets lost in the hustle and bustle of everyday life. Because it is always with you, it colors your life through your emotions and moods. Subconsciously, you are absorbing information from it all day long. This is how we get gut feelings. Our subconscious sends us intuitive information, and suddenly something hits us as being "off." Or we feel incredibly drawn to people or situations. Most of the time, this is how our intuition communicates with us.

Now, however, we wish to access our intuition at the conscious level. We want answers to specific questions. We want information around the issues we are working on right now. And so we sit down and dowse, or use muscle testing. Essentially, we are turning up the volume on that radio. And invariably, we're a little disappointed. *"This can't be my intuition,"* we think. *"I already knew all that."* The little voice inside of us is just like our own. The feelings we receive when we tune in to our internal intuitive perception are just like what we feel every day. If we hear sounds or have words pop into our heads, it's probably nothing that doesn't happen all the time. It's nothing earth-shattering at all. There are no lightning bolts, no striking visions that remove us completely from reality. No booming voice resounds in our heads, gifting us with startling revelations that change our lives. That's the Hollywood version, but that's not how it really happens! The voice of your Higher Self is gentle, affirming, and uplifting. It is not upsetting, and it does not turn your life upside down.

Your intuition is quiet and familiar. Your intuition is a part of you, and always has been. You've been accessing it unconsciously every day of your life. The difference is that now you've started taking notice. When you consciously tune into that little voice and those small feelings, trust them!

IMAGINATION AS A TOOL

Let's have another look at the imagination. What is imagination, really, but a tool by which to access non-ordinary reality? Let me describe what I mean: You are sitting in a restaurant, looking at a menu. You now actively use your imagination to access a possible future in which you are eating, say, a bacon cheeseburger. Your imagination supplies information from that possible future such as taste, how full you'll feel after your meal, etc. Your conscious mind then decides whether this possible future is desirable or not, and orders food accordingly. But your imagination just went and accessed a reality that does not exist in the present moment—hence, non-ordinary reality. Your imagination does this at your command all the time. Your imagination travels back to past events, rewrites them, accesses probable and improbable future scenarios, and is an integral part of your decision-making and learning process. Your imagination is the means by which you travel to places and circumstances that do not exist in your physical reality at the moment in which you are imagining them.

If the imagination is the means by which people access information that does not exist in current reality, is it a surprise that intuition would come in through the same channel of communication? This is why imagination and intuition feel so alarmingly similar. Both access information that is not available to the conscious mind from its third-dimensional surroundings.

If you imagine by seeing whole movies in your head, chances are that your intuition will also give you very visual images. If you imagine by having a running narrative in your mind, your intuition will also probably be a continuous verbal stream. If you listen to or feel your imagination at work, most likely your intuition will also be heard or felt. Most of us access more than one sensory level when we use our imaginations. So, the next time you day-dream, pay close attention to how you access that particular non-ordinary reality. It is a huge clue to how your internal intuitive perception will play out.

EXERCISE

For the next five minutes, take a little vacation in your mind. Imagine what it would be like if one of your desired outcomes were to manifest itself into your current reality. Enjoy this experience! At the same time, notice how you place yourself into this scenario. Then write down a detailed account of the experience of your imagination. How does your imagination work? Do you imagine visually, verbally, auditory, or kinesthetically? About what percentage of each do you employ? Which resonates most deeply with you? Which creates the greatest emotional reaction?

TELLING IMAGINATION FROM INTUITION

The big question is, of course, *how do you tell imagination from intuition?* There is a subtle but distinctive difference between the two that will serve to guide you in separating one from the other.

Imagine all the goings-on in your mind as a play, if you will. There are scenes playing themselves out and actors saying their lines. Perhaps there's a running narrative going on. Perhaps you hear sound-effects, people talking, and so forth. Perhaps you feel yourself as part of the play.

When you are using your imagination, your conscious mind is the director of the play. When you were reading that menu, your conscious mind told your imagination to go and access information about what it would be like to eat a bacon cheeseburger. When you are day-dreaming about your ideal job, your conscious mind is telling your imagination to access that non-ordinary reality. You may not always feel in charge of this process—sometimes we catch ourselves day-dreaming, after all. But your mind is still in charge. You may not always be in charge of your mind ... but that's a whole other issue we're not going to tackle. What is important to recognize is that the conscious mind, the thinking part of you, is directing the play that is taking place in your head. Whatever shape that play may take for you—kinesthetic, visual, verbal or auditory—your thinking mind is running the show.

When you are using your intuition, your conscious mind is the audience. When you are receiving intuitive information, your conscious mind is doing exactly that—receiving. Your conscious mind is like the audience member, merely witnessing the play. It is passively observing the information that is coming from your Higher Self. Its only active role is to pose the questions. Your conscious mind does not participate in creating the answers. When you are using your intuition, the answers will resonate in your being without any mental effort. That's why you may doubt the validity of the information at times—receiving it will be very easy. The job of the conscious mind is to be open and receptive.

All of your divination practice so far has served an additional goal: your conscious mind is now practiced at posing a question, and then going into a receptive state in order to receive the answer. We have spent so much time in our divination practice circumventing the conscious mind that it has been trained to stay out of the way. Now, if you have decided to take a few short-cuts and not put in the suggested amount of practice time, you may at this point want to decide to back up a few steps. Do not short-change yourself within this process. Everything we have done up to now has served to create a solid foundation upon which to build your intuitive abilities.

THE IMPORTANCE OF PROCESS

Finally, one other aspect of this methodology assures that you can be confident in the information you receive—your consistent log-on process! Remember that we created a process to use at the beginning of each session to ensure that your answers are coming from your Higher Self through your subconscious mind. If you've gotten careless about using your log-on process, go back, memorize it, and spend the next few days being very consistent.

While you've been dowsing and muscle testing, a clear system of communication has been created in the interaction between your Higher Self, your subconscious, and your conscious mind. Your Higher Self gives the answer, which your subconscious relays to your body. Your conscious mind receives the information through the swing of the pendulum, or the muscular reactions of your body. Notice that the conscious mind has been in a receptive state since we began this journey. We are now internalizing this same process. Consistency is a key element in maintaining the receptive state that the conscious mind has become accustomed to.

In our initial log-on process, we also direct our intention to access information from our Higher Self. That is a very key element when we start relying less on divination, and more on our internal intuitive perception. The intention of accessing our Higher Self creates a state of openness and receptivity within the conscious mind, and ensures that the information is coming from the appropriate source.

EXERCISE

Ask at least ten questions of your Higher Self. Using your work with your imagination as your guide, actively look for the internal aspect of the answers resonating within you. Maintain a relaxed and receptive state within your conscious mind, allowing it to be the observer. Once you have clear internal reception of your answers, you may want to delay divination, using your pendulum or muscle testing only to confirm the answers you received internally.

CREATING YOUR SACRED SPACE

Your intuitive process is part of your everyday spiritual practice. While you will certainly be able to eventually access this tool while engaged in other activities, it can be helpful to create a sacred space in which to conduct your intuitive inquiries. This doesn't require a separate room in your house. A corner of your bedroom, or even just a meditation pillow, can become your sacred space. I personally like to play meditative, soothing music while I work. I also always light a candle, because to me this represents Divine Light, through which we connect to Spirit. You can also burn incense or create a small altar of meaningful objects to designate your sacred space. The point is to create a consistent setting for your intuitive practice. This is your special place to retreat, go inward and connect to your Higher Self. By working with your intuition in the same environment, playing the same music, lighting the same incense or candle, you are further using the elements of ritual and repetition to create the appropriate state of mind to receive accurate intuitive information. Even in the midst of emotional or mental turmoil, your sacred space will become a place of peace and clarity where you can access the wisdom and guidance of the spiritual plane.

GOING INWARD

Through the previous exercises in this chapter, you should now have a clear sense of how your intuition resonates internally. If you do not, I highly advise you to continue dowsing with *"yes"* and *"no"* questions, asking at least ten or twenty questions of your Higher Self every day. This internal awareness comes with time and practice. Once this awareness is achieved, we can start shifting our focus from the external method of divination to our internal receptors for intuitive information!

Hold on, though—don't put your pendulum out to pasture just yet! As we begin accessing a free information flow, we will continue to use our method of divination to confirm the information we receive. As you move towards open-ended questions, I advise you to use your divination method to ensure that both your questions and answers are in alignment with Divine Truth. This is especially true if you receive answers that surprise you. Divination is a very reliable, easy way to ensure accuracy. There will be days when you are tired, feeling emotional, in a hurry, or unfocused and just want a quick and easy answer. Remember that you can always return to the simplicity of *"yes"* and *"no"* questions.

I also hope that you have put some of the intuitive information to use in your life, and have developed some confidence and faith in the answers you receive. Having trust in the work that you have already accomplished will greatly serve you in the next part of the intuitive development process.

If you are not sure that you're ready for open-ended questions, you may at this point ask your Higher Self!

* *Is it in alignment with my desired outcome of developing reliable, consistent, and accurate access to my intuition to proceed towards asking open-ended questions?*

If the answer to this question is negative, you might want to ask for probable time frames within which you will need to continue practicing. If the answer is positive, move forward with confidence!

ೞ

Chapter Six

Beyond Yes or No

– Accessing the Information Flow

By now, you will have developed an excellent sense of how your internal intuitive perception works. You probably know with quite a high degree of accuracy what the answer will be well before you use your method of divination. You know what *"yes"* and *"no"* feels like, sounds like, or looks like internally. So far, however, your internal intuitive receptors have only had these two possible answers to choose from. We now want to open ourselves up to receiving more extensive information from our Higher Self.

CREATING A CLEAR CHANNEL OF COMMUNICATION

Through careful observation, you've learned a great deal about how intuitive information is most naturally inclined to enter your conscious mind. You have discovered the predominant inherent tendencies you have towards visual, auditory, verbal, or kinesthetic intuitive perception. It is now time to establish a clear channel of communication with your Higher Self that takes into account both your natural tendencies and the practical aspects of receiving intuitive information.

We know what our natural inclinations are in the way we perceive information from our Higher Self, but we may find that one way of receiving answers is less confusing or more practical than others. I personally receive information verbally and kinesthetically. In my work with my clients, however, I find it most practical to receive intuitive information through a predominantly verbal channel of communication. This allows me to relay information verbatim to my clients, exactly the way it came from the spiritual plane, rather than having to interpret kinesthetic cues through my own perspective and frame of reference. And so that is how I prefer to receive my intuitive information: words just pop into my head!

You may, for instance, love watching movies in your head, whereas kinesthetic information is harder for you to interpret. Therefore, you may request to receive your intuitive information primarily through visual cues. Or perhaps you find visual images too hard to focus on, and love hearing the answers in your head. In any case, among your natural tendencies, you may find that you have a preference for how you wish to receive information.

Now that you know your natural inclinations in receiving intuitive information, and have had experience with this phenomenon, we want to create a definite intention for communicating with our Higher Self. This will be tremendously helpful to your Higher Self. Instead of having to work very hard in order to get its information across, it knows what channel of communication is open and expected. Your Higher Self will connect with you far more efficiently through a consciously designated method of contact.

You might think that your Higher Self, with its access to all that insight, information, and wisdom, would know what is best for you, and would simply act accordingly. This is not necessarily true. The Higher Self is the aspect of you that resides in the spiritual plane. As we mentioned earlier, it does not always consider the practical necessities of the physical plane. Consider yourself the manger of the connection between your physical aspect and your spiritual resources.

In defining your channel of communication, you must work with your natural tendencies of inner perception. If you are a very kinesthetic person, please don't try to receive only verbal cues, just because this might seem more practical to you!

EXERCISE: *Define a clear channel of communication with your Higher Self.*

Step 1: Write down your natural tendencies in receiving intuitive information. Are you primarily visual, with a little bit of kinesthetic awareness thrown into the mix? Are you mostly auditory, with a few visual cues? Describe what happens for you when you receive intuitive information internally.

Step 2: Of all the ways you naturally receive intuitive information internally, which is the easiest and clearest for you? Do you like seeing a movie unfold in front of you, whereas auditory messages confuse you? Or do you like hearing your Higher Self talk to you, while kinesthetic messages just distract you? Write down which cues offer you the clearest, most easily perceived information.

Step 3: Write down how you would like to receive intuitive information. Be very precise. Describe the volume, the clarity, the tone of voice of the information that you want. Describe exactly how you would like to perceive it. Do you want to see images in color, or in black and white? Do you want them to be sharp and defined, or fuzzy and dreamlike? Again, use your natural tendencies as a starting point. But be clear! The more defined this description is, the better. When you define the communication channel in this way, it will also help you recognize intuitive information when your Higher Self is trying to communicate with you.

Step 4: Define your intention.

> *Creator of all Beings (x3), Divine Archangels (x3), my personal Team of Guides, Teachers, and Angels(x3), my Higher Self, my Conscious Self, my Subconscious Self (x3) …*
>
> *I hereby state my intention to create a clear channel of communication with my Higher Self, using the following guidelines. Communication will be initiated by the following process:*
>
> *I will inhale to the count of four, hold my breath to the count of four, and exhale to the count of eight. I will repeat this breath for a total of three times to create a surcharge of vital force. I will then say: "In the name of Truth and Love and Light, let all information come from my Higher Self, in alignment with Divine Truth for my Highest Good and the Highest Good of all Beings everywhere. Thank you, thank you, thank you."*
>
> *I will request intuitive information through questions that are in alignment with Divine Truth. It is my intention to receive all information from my Higher Self following the initial process stated above through the following set of internal perceptors:*
>
> *(Give your detailed description of your communication channel here.)*
>
> *I will end each session by thanking my Higher Self and announcing that I am closing the conscious channel of communication.*
>
> *For my highest good and the highest good of all, I command this intention to be carried out with joy. Thank you, thank you, thank you."*

You have now created very clear parameters for how you wish to receive intuitive information from your Higher Self. Not only will this allow your Higher Self to focus its energy into this specific channel of communication, it will also make it much easier for you to identify intuitive information as it enters your consciousness.

TURNING INTUITION ON AND OFF

There is an additional reason we included the log-on process we've been using since we first started with divination in the above statement of intent. You don't want to walk through life with your antennas up, an open conduit to intuitive information at all times. This can be very disruptive to your every day life, not to mention hazardous while driving or chopping vegetables. Being always *"on"* can lead to trouble concentrating, disrupted sleep patterns, a lack of focus, or becoming overwhelmed by the amount of information coming in. At times, your Higher Self may also have quite important information to relay to you. If that information comes in at random, when you are barely aware of it because you are busy with life, it may be ignored. Instead, give yourself the opportunity to access your intuition when you can give the information the attention it deserves.

When you turn your intuition *"on,"* you are expecting information from your Higher Self. This will help you distinguish it further from your imagination. Note that we also stated that we would request intuitive information specifically by asking questions. This will also be a tool for you to manage the information flow. We don't just want to receive random information that may or may not be useful to us at this time. Later on in this book, when we have become very comfortable with open-ended questions, we may ask: *"What is really important for me to know today?"* But once again, we will have accessed the information through our conscious intent by asking a question.

Just as we log on to our Higher Self, we will also now start "logging off." We will do this by simply thanking our Higher Self and announcing that we are done with our session. Previously, you simply put your pendulum away or ended your muscle testing, and the process was complete. Now that you are creating this internal connection, you want to be sure that your Higher Self knows when you are done receiving information.

Consider yourself as having an "always on" high speed Internet connection to your Higher Self. While the connection is always there, you do have to open your browser to access the Web. And you also have to put in the appropriate web address or URL, or run a search on the right terms to find the information you want. And, when you are done, you would normally close the browser, because this protects you from unwanted intrusions such as pop-ups and spyware.

It is the same with accessing your intuition. Log on, ask your questions, and don't forget to log off when you're done. The last part, as simple as it is, is often easily forgotten. If you find yourself walking around in a daze, you've probably forgotten to "log off!" Important as initiating the process of accessing your intuition is, it is equally important to consciously complete your intuitive process. We are creating boundaries and distinction in your life between being in ordinary conscious reality, and accessing your intuition. The more the lines between the two blur, the harder it will be to distinguish intuition from mere imagination. Through the process of logging on and off, receiving information from your Higher Self becomes a clearly defined, conscious activity. Your intuition will be a tool that you access on your own terms, as needed and desired. With time and practice, logging on and off will take you no time at all. It may seem tedious at first, but repetition and consistency will let this process become second nature to you very quickly.

Down the road, you may wish to ask your Higher Self if you can abbreviate this process. Be sure to work with your Higher Self on defining your short-cuts. Do not rush into this step. Practice with the process you just created for at least six months. Lay a firm foundation now, and it will serve you for a long time to come. As you become more accomplished, you will be able to access your intuition while performing other activities—in line at the grocery store, folding laundry, and so on. Accessing your intuition will become se   nature, but you will always be consciously in charge of the process.

ASKING OPEN-ENDED QUESTIONS

Finally, we are ready to ask open-ended questions! Once again—and I know I sound like a broken record!—it is important that you can clearly sense *"yes"* or *"no"* internally before proceeding. We have discussed the importance of maintaining a clear and distinct process for the beginning and ending of your sessions, and now you're almost ready to start! A few things to consider before you launch into your actual questions:

◆ *It is extremely difficult to remember all the details of the information you receive from an open-ended question.* Remember, your conscious mind is in a fairly passive, observant state. This can make it very difficult to recall the exact answers you are given. I highly advise having some way to record your answers handy. You can either write down the information you are receiving as it comes in, or speak it into a tape recorder as you receive it. Both methods have worked nicely for me in the past. If you work best with your eyes closed because you receive visual messages in your mind's eye, a tape recorder may serve you best. If you receive verbal or auditory communications, writing them down verbatim may work well for you.

◆ *Be specific in your questioning.* You've already learned this skill from formulating *"yes"* and *"no"* questions, but still maintain awareness around the quality of your questions. If you are unsure of the quality of the question, ask your Higher Self: *"Is this question in alignment with Divine Truth? Is this question appropriately worded in order to align with Divine Truth? Is it appropriate for me to ask this question at this time?"* It can be as important to research your questions as it is to research the answers. The more general your question, the less specific your answer will be. For now, I recommend continuing with the frames of reference I outlined in

Chapter Four about questioning, until you gain more confidence and your Higher Self can teach you new appropriate frames of reference.

♦ *Information from your Higher Self, and later on, your Spirit Guides, will always be positive and uplifting.* The information will always be supportive, inspiring, helpful, and enlightening. It will never be derogatory, critical, confusing, or cryptic. Your Higher Self will never demand a radical life change of you. Your Higher Self and your Spirit Guides will not give you information that you cannot understand. They are eager and willing to help you and be a resource to you. Their job is not to be mysterious! If you receive information outside of these guidelines, it is most likely not coming from the appropriate sources. If you have followed all of the processes I have outlined in this book so far, it is highly unlikely that you will intuitively connect to any negative entities. It would take an incredibly strong negative being to hijack your channel of communication. Still, this is not outside of the realm of possibility. Should you encounter difficulties in this area, please consult Chapter Eight of this book.

♦ *Your Higher Self and your Spirit Guides will never tell you what to do.* I know we would sometimes like them to make our decisions on our behalf. However, they are only responsible for giving us information that our conscious mind does not have access to. It is up to us to decide what to do with this information. The responsibility of choice and free will falls to us.

OPEN-ENDED QUESTIONS

Asking an open-ended question can be a little daunting. *"Yes"* and *"no"* have become easy and comfortable. Now you are opening yourself up to receiving information without having any prior notion of what those answers may be. It may take a little time and getting used to. We are going to integrate our divination method and *"yes"* and *"no"* answers into the open-ended questioning process, until we get truly comfortable. Make sure you have your pendulum at hand!

Before you proceed further, please complete your log-on process at this time. Then let's start with a universally helpful question:

⬥ *What is my primary life lesson chosen for this lifetime?*

I think this is something everyone should know about themselves! Our Souls choose a specific subject to study for this lifetime. Other secondary life lessons will usually support the understanding of the primary life lesson. This is a great question to start with because you will be able to confirm the validity of the information, based on your life experiences. Life lessons often present themselves as challenges and obstacles. If the answer is *"Integrity in Love"* and you've had a great many challenges within this area, then the information is no doubt correct.

Ask the question, out loud or in your thoughts.

⬥ *What is my primary life lesson chosen for this lifetime?*

What is your first impulse? Given the parameters you set for your preferred mode of internal perception, what is the first thing that leaps into your mind? What is the very first impression you receive?

Let's say, for instance, what leaps into your head is something like *"unity, unification, union ..."* Now you can ask your Higher Self, using your divination method:

⬥ *Does my primary life lesson have something to do with the concept of unity? Unification? Union?*

If you receive a *"no"* answer on all of these, ask the first questions again and tune in to your internal preceptors for the first impulse you receive. This can take some practice. Be patient with yourself! If you receive a *"yes"* answer to the concept of *"unity,"* for example, you know you're on the right track. So now we want some clarification. You can ask your Higher Self:

⬥ *My primary life lesson is unity between ... ?*

See what your next impulse is. You might receive an answer such as *"unity within relationships," "unity of body and spirit,"* or *"creating unity within organizations."* Keep confirming with your Higher Self using your divination method. For instance, if your first impulse has something to do with Spirit and the concept of *"all,"* you might ask:

⬧ *Is my primary life lesson "unity of spirit between all living things?"*

This is where you will really rely on your inner preceptors of intuitive information for guidance. Feel free to clarify and to narrow down your definition as much as you feel is necessary. Confirm with a *"yes"* or *"no"* question every step of the way.

In the beginning, this will seem like a tedious process for many of you. For some of you, complete answers may leap into your mind immediately. For most of us, it takes a little more practice. However, the more open-ended questions you ask, the quicker this process will become. After a while, you will receive a complete answer with a single question.

The questions you can ask now are only limited by your imagination. However, because of the vastness of information available to you, it may be difficult to know where to start. Below are some possible open-ended questions aligning with Divine Truth that may serve you.

⬧ *To what percentage am I complete with my primary life lesson for this lifetime?*

⬧ *What is my purpose for this lifetime? To what percentage am I aligned with it?*

⬧ *In what areas of my life is this life lesson currently manifesting itself? How is it manifesting itself?*

⬧ *What life lesson is attached to the experience of … that I am currently having?*

- *Is a decision within a specific life area necessary at this time to move me forward on my highest path and purpose? Which life area? What choices are available, and which is most in alignment with my highest path and purpose?*

- *What avenues of possibility are available to me right now that will move me towards my desired outcome of...?*

- *What Soul-level gifts and talents do I possess that I am currently not utilizing?*

- *How many past lifetimes have I lived?*

- *What past life history, if any, do I share with this person?*

- *What probable outcome will this decision bring within the next two weeks? Two months? Two years? To what percentage is this outcome probable?*

- *Within what time frame would this action be most likely to take me towards my desired outcome?*

- *What opportunities are available to manifest my Soul purpose within my current career path? What people in my life can assist me?*

- *How do I attract the appropriate people that will assist me in moving towards my desired outcome?*

If you are stuck for which question to ask, your Higher Self can help you with this also.

- *What life area would it be most helpful for me to ask questions about today?*

- *Is there a frame of reference I am not familiar with that would assist me in obtaining more helpful information about this subject at this present time?*

♦ *What is this frame of reference?* (Please note that this is a fairly advanced process. A new frame of reference for you means that you really have no prior conscious knowledge of what your Higher Self is talking about! However, sometimes these are the most useful and fascinating topics to research!)

Let your Higher Self be your teacher in the appropriate wording of questions. You will find as you work within this process that you will be guided in your questioning as much as in the answers you receive. With a little diligent practice, the appropriate questions will leap into your mind as much as the answers do. When this happens, you will find that your communication with your Higher Self takes on the energy and flow of an enlightening, inspiring, easy conversation with a good friend and wise mentor. This is the goal we have been moving towards in this book.

EXERCISE

For the next two weeks, ask at least five open-ended questions every day of your Higher Self, using questions that align with Divine Truth. Keep a journal of the questions asked, and the corresponding answers you receive.

Once you are comfortable in communicating with your Higher Self, and the questions and answers are flowing easily into your conscious mind through your internal intuitive preceptors, do not be surprised if you notice that your Higher Self has a real personality! You may encounter light-hearted humor, a little impatience when you ask a question more than once, and a great deal of unconditional love and compassion. Your Higher Self will become a valuable collaborator in embracing your Soul's highest path and purpose. Your Higher Self will truly serve you as an amazing resource on your path of spiritual growth.

☙

CHAPTER SEVEN

WORKING WITH DISCORPORATE ENTITIES

–SPIRITUAL GUIDES, TEACHERS, AND GRANDMA

There are many, many discorporate entities and Souls about us at any given time. In fact, there are more entities and Souls in our plane of existence that are currently not occupying a physical body than there are Souls in body! These non-physical entities include our Spirit Guides, other spiritual guides and teachers, earthbound spirits, ghosts, poltergeists, and psychic entities. Some of these entities are a great resource to our spiritual development. Others may be positive spirits, but really don't have much guidance to offer us. Others are negative, and will make an effort to mislead and misguide us.

Have no doubt that as you work with your Higher Self and your intuitive perception expands, you will become aware of these entities. As your intuitive senses sharpen, all kinds of discorporate beings will try to get your attention. Some may be genuinely invested in your growth, like your Spirit Guides. Some may be sent to you by Spirit as an additional resource. Some may just be bored and want to interact—just like you'd have an idle conversation in line at the grocery store. Others will try to create mischief or harm. This chapter is designed to help you tell the difference.

I cannot stress enough how important it is that you know who you are speaking with. There is such a thrill and fascination that comes with having interaction with discorporate entities for the first time! Many whose intuition is just opening up are willing to believe that they are communicating with Archangels, Jesus himself, or their dearly departed grandma—without ever questioning the entity they are communicating with. I'm not trying to invalidate their experience, which can be very personally meaningful. I do, however, advise caution when it comes to communicating with discorporate beings.

If someone walked up to you on the street and started talking to you, what would your first instinct be? My first questions would be *"Who the heck are you? Is it safe for me to talk to you? And why should I listen to anything you have to say?"* If that person identified themselves as an authority, you'd ask for credentials, right? You'd ask a police officer for his or her badge, for instance. Just because an entity is not in body right now doesn't mean the same rules don't apply. We want to know who they are, why they are contacting us, and why we should listen. There are some people who are willing to communicate with just about any entity that comes along. This can not only be a complete waste of time, it can be downright dangerous! Please be discerning about which beings you communicate with. Just as you wouldn't trust a stranger you met on the street, do not automatically trust a discorporate entity that contacts you for a chat.

BASIC DISCERNMENT – NEGATIVE OR POSITIVE ENTITY?

The very, very first thing you must ascertain when you open yourself up to communication with a discorporate entity is whether they are a positive or negative being. I cannot stress enough how important this is!

Positive beings are aligned with Divine Love, Light, and Truth. They are on a path of Soul evolution and work with Divine Light energy as their source of vital force. Positive entities and Souls thrive on positive energies, such as love, happiness, joy, trust, confidence, and so forth. Negative influences may attach to them, but their nature is oriented towards Light. Their Souls are pursuing growth and development towards the ultimate goal of enlightenment. These beings are safe, if not necessarily always helpful, to speak with.

Negative beings, on the other hand, are on a path of de-evolution. They have chosen to work with negative energies as a source of vital force. Much as positive Souls thrive on love and happiness, negative entities derive their power from anger, fear, hatred, shame, blame, guilt, and other negative energies. The problem for negative entities is, however, that ***there is no source of dark energy in our Universe!*** Source only generates Divine Light. Negative entities therefore need to create negativity within positive Souls. They need to generate negativity within others, because they do not have any other source of power. They are therefore constantly seeking to attach and create negative interference energy—because this is how they survive. These negative entities and Souls have chosen to work with a different quality of energy than positive Souls. We do not judge this—we simply seek to disallow it when they attempt to draw on our vital force by creating negative influences in our lives.

Negative entities have just one job to do—to create negative energies within you, so that they can become stronger. They do this through misinformation, creating confusion and upheaval. At the same time, this deprives you of vital force energy, and creates a lot of negativity in your life. We therefore do not engage with negative entities, in any way. And we have all the power in the world to avoid negative entities!

All dark, or negative, energy is really just the absence of Light. What makes negative energy so powerful is our belief in it. In reality, if we turn on our Light, darkness has no choice but to go away. Just like throwing a switch and turning a light on in a dark room, darkness immediately is obliterated. In other words, positive beings always have power over negative beings. And this is why there is nothing to be afraid of here. This is also why negative entities and Souls have to resort to trickery and deception in order to influence us. No negative entity that contacts you is ever going to look nasty and say *"Hey, I'm up to no good, come talk to me!"* Instead, they will pose as helpful and wise teachers, or even as your departed loved ones.

So, our first task when communicating with entities of any kind is to throw on the light switch! Before you enter into any kind of communication, your first question must be:

⬧ *Is your Soul Being in alignment with Divine Love, Light, and Truth?*

The response here should be a resounding, emphatic and immediate *"YES!"* This identifies a positive entity. This is an entity that is at least safe, if not necessarily helpful, to talk to.

If you receive no response, a question in response to your own, an evasive answer, or anything other than a definite positive response, this entity is negative. Very few negative entities will answer with an immediate *"no."* They will usually try to wriggle out of a direct answer. Do not engage in further contact with them. Their communication will always be full of misdirection and will not assist you on your path to Soul growth. Ask your Spirit Guides and Higher Self to disallow all further communication or association with this particular entity. Remember that you, as a currently incarnated Soul, have all the power. You're the one with access to vital force energy in this dimension. If you tell them to go away and disallow all further contact, they must obey you.

YOUR SPIRIT GUIDES

Our Spirit Guides are one of the greatest resources we can draw upon. Below is an outline of the structure of your spiritual committee.

THE STRUCTURE OF YOUR SPIRITUAL COMMITTEE

The Spirit Guides that are assigned to you currently for this lifetime are divided into two groups: the Inner Circle and the Outer Circle of Guides.

Your *Inner Circle of Guides* are your very own personal Spirit Guides, exclusively assigned to assist you on your journey in this lifetime. We have a highly intimate relationship with our Inner Circle of Spirit Guides. If our Higher Self can be regarded as our parent aspect on the spiritual plane, then our Spirit Guides are the caring aunts and uncles that are deeply invested in our growth and well-being. The primary role of our Guides is to offer us information from a more varied perspective than our Higher Self alone can access. Our Spirit Guides come from a slightly more advanced aspect of Soul evolution than our Higher Self. Our Spirit Guides have their own history, life experiences, and Soul-level gifts and talents to draw upon. Each Guide has its own unique perspective through which it offers us guidance. In the physical, we have many teachers and mentors beyond our parents. Similarly, we are offered a broad range of assistance and information through our Spirit Guides on the spiritual plane.

Usually, there are four to six Guides present in your Inner Circle. These guides have usually incarnated into the Earth plane previously. They are familiar with the physical plane (although they may have forgotten some of the concepts of the physical world—or these concepts may have changed since their last incarnation). This is what makes them so effective in assisting us. Your Guides have had experience in the physical, but now can offer us the perspective of the spiritual plane, as well as their own areas of knowledge and expertise in order to assist us. In guiding us, our Guides are contributing to their own Soul growth and development. Their presence in our lives is their current assignment in working on behalf of Spirit.

Your Inner Circle of Guides is around you all the time. One of them has been with you from birth. You will have "hired" the others as you have progressed through childhood and adolescence into early adulthood. These loving helpers are around you to assist you in every day life and work exclusively on your behalf, and they are the guides you will work with and talk to the most.

Our Spirit Guides are the only non-physical entities that have direct interaction with us while we are incarnated. All other entities must have our permission, at least at the unconscious level, in order to communicate with us. Our Spirit Guides, however, can seek to influence us and initiate communication as they see fit, in alignment with our highest path and purpose. Not only do they work with our Higher Self on the spiritual plane, they also work with us directly here in the physical. ach of our Spirit Guides impulses us in a certain way. The impulse can be through a physical sensation, a scent, a thought pattern, or a specific feeling. This is how our Spirit Guides seek our attention. Through these impulses, they make their presence known and offer us their guidance. For example, I have a Spirit Guide that impulses me with a tingling on my upper left arm and elbow that always gives me goosebumps. This is how I know that he is present and is trying to get my attention. I also once had a client with a Spirit Guide who impulsed her by making her toes twitch. When I relayed this information to her, she started laughing because she is forever taking off her shoes and her toes are constantly in motion. She had always wondered about her oddly overactive toes. As it turns out, her Spirit Guide was trying to communicate with her.

This process of being impulsed remains largely unconscious for most of us. However, now that you are able to ask open-ended questions, you can ask each of your Guides for the specific impulse by which they make their presence known. In this way, you can begin to pay more conscious attention to their guidance in your life.

Because they are around you all the time and their presence is very familiar, you will probably need to make a conscious effort to tune in to your Guides. They are most likely not the entities that will make themselves known first—not because they are not engaged with you, but because you have worked with them for so long that their presence has become second-nature to you.

While our Guides certainly have a wealth of information to offer us, we can also ask them to take action on our behalf. We must request their assistance consciously, however, in order for them to actively support our goals. Our Guides cannot take action on our behalf on their own initiative, because this would interfere with our free will and free choice. This is why I always include Spirit Guides in any prayer request. If we consciously request their aid, our Spirit Guides are able to assist us in manifesting our desired outcomes. They can coordinate further assistance for us from the various angelic realms. Our Spirit Guides themselves can also lend energetic support to any of our life situations.

Your *Outer Circle of Guides* is very busy—they have more than one "client" at a time. There are seven guides present in your outer circle, each in charge of a specific area of your life. Your Outer Circle is made up of much older souls, usually far more spiritually advanced than us, with many, many times our spiritual life experience to draw upon. They are therefore less involved in the small details of our everyday lives. They can be seen as "upper-level management" when it comes to our spiritual evolution, whereas our Inner Circle are our "hands-on" team that works with us at a more intimate level.

1) **YOUR CHIEF GUIDE**—coordinates your Inner and Outer Circles, as well as our spiritual masters, teachers and special assignment guides. He's the manager in charge, so to speak.

2) **YOUR GATEKEEPER**—is in charge of opening your memory files at the appropriate times. He is in charge of the collection of your experiences

and knowledge over lifetimes, and on presenting you with the path appropriate with your purpose and mission for this current lifetime.

3) **YOUR TIMING GUIDE**—works closely with the gatekeeper and is in charge of creating the timing of the most appropriate experiences for you.

4) **YOUR KARMIC TECH**—is responsible for helping you resolve unfinished business and completing karma accumulated in past and present lifetimes.

5) **YOUR CREATIVE ONE**—facilitates talents and connects you to beauty and aesthetics. The area of specialty of this guide can give us clues as to your creative talent.

6) **YOUR ASHER**—is your bodyguard, and is best left alone! This is one guide I would advise you not to contact. This guide is responsible for your physical safety, and you do not want to distract him.

7) **YOUR ASTRAL GUIDE**—accompanies and guides you during your astral (sleep) time and helps you travel and return to your body safely.

There is little need for communicating directly with your Outer Circle on a daily basis. Contacting your Chief Guide is the equivalent of contacting the CEO of a large corporation, when what you really need is the Customer Service Department. Be discerning about reaching out to your Outer Circle. Your Inner Circle interacts with your Outer Circle on your behalf as needed. For example, if a current life situation needs a specific timeline in the physical in order to fall into place, your Inner Circle Guides will work with your Timing Guide on this matter. Your Higher Self will also reach out to your Outer Circle Guides for assistance or information, if necessary. You will rarely need to pose a question to your Outer Circle directly.

OPENING A CHANNEL OF COMMUNICATION WITH YOUR GUIDES

Once you've become comfortable with the process of asking open-ended questions and receiving answers, it will be relatively easy to establish communication with your Spirit Guide Team. You may use the following process:

Initiate your log-on process as you do for every session of intuitive inquiry.

Ask your Inner Circle of Guides to step forward, one at a time. Be specific, so that you can be sure you are contacting the right group of entities. Ask the Number One Guide of your Inner Circle to step forward and make him/her/itself known. Your Guides will usually line up in the order in which you hired them, so your Number One Guide is usually (but not always) the Guide that was with you at birth. When you feel a presence as having presented itself, you need to take some steps to ensure that you are, indeed, talking to the right entity! Ask if the entity is aligned with Divine Love, Light, and Truth. You should get an immediate and positive response. Remember, if there is no response, or an unclear response, you are talking to a negative entity and should immediately cease communication!

Once your apparent Spirit Guide has affirmed that they are aligned with Divine Love, Light, and Truth, ask whether they are indeed part of your Inner Circle. Your Guides won't take offense at this—they understand and support that you need to be sure who you are talking to. Once you have established that you are talking to the appropriate entity, the following questions can help you get to know your Inner Circle Guide better:

*   *What is your name?*
*   *Can you give me a visual impression of your appearance?*
*   *What is your special area of focus on my team?*
*   *How do you impulse me?*
*   *What specific message do you have for me?*

You may receive a great deal of information through these questions. Some Guides will be more communicative than others. Be prepared to record the information you receive. Expect your Guides to have quite distinct personalities. They often have a wonderful sense of humor, and encourage us not to take ourselves too seriously. Laughter is a gift from Spirit, and your Guides will usually be a pretty joyous bunch. They may also have unusual appearances. Don't be surprised if your Guides look like something out of a science fiction movie, or present as a geometric shape or even just a blob of color. Some of your Guides may not give you a name. Sometimes they have moved beyond the confines of language and identify themselves merely through their energetic signature.

Your Guides will *not* be Souls that have crossed over during your present lifetime. While Souls of departed loved ones such as deceased parents, grandparents, or others who were close to you in life may from time to time contact you to give you guidance, they will not be a part of your Inner Guide circle. You may have shared a physical past life with some of your Guides, but you will not have known each other in the physical in your present lifetime. If one of your Guides on your Inner Circle identifies itself as a departed loved one, you may be receiving misinformation, or are not clear enough in your intention and have contacted the wrong entity.

Information from your Guides will always be positive, loving, and uplifting. There will never be any criticism, guilt, or negativity coming from your team. Your Guides will never, ever tell you what to do. They know that the power and responsibility of choice always lies with you, in the conscious mind.

Once you've established communication with each of your Guides, you may want to ask one of them to step forward and act as a representative for your team. That way, if you wish to ask your Guide team a question, you do not have to communicate and receive answers from four to six separate entities—that is quite a lot of work and can be time consuming. Instead, one Guide can act as a "spokesguide" for your entire Inner Circle. Often, this "spokesguide" will be the Guide that was assigned to you at birth. However, once you know what each Guide's area of specialty is on your team, you may direct requests for information or assistance to that specific Guide.

YOUR GUIDES AND YOUR HIGHER SELF

For the sake of expediency, unless you want input specifically from your Guides, I would advise you to continue to direct your general questions to your Higher Self. Your Higher Self usually consults with your Guide team when giving you answers. You can regard your Higher Self as the manager of your resources on the spiritual plane. When you access your Higher Self, you also automatically access the wisdom of your Guide team.

SPIRITUAL MASTERS AND TEACHERS, AND ANGELS

On occasion, additional guides, teachers and angels from the spiritual plane will present themselves. As always, it is important to establish that these entities are positive before agreeing to communicate with them. Once you've established that the entity is positive, you will want to find out what dimension they are from. This will establish how helpful these entities will be to you. The following chart outlines the various dimensions of the spiritual plane:

Dimension	Beings
4th Dimension	Humans, Animal and Plant Kingdom
5th Dimension	Humans and Spirit Guides
6th Dimension	Spirit Guides
7th Dimension	Masters and Teachers
8th Dimension	Master Teachers (Jesus, Buddha, Krishna)
9th Dimension	Worker and Guardian Angels
10th & 11th Dimension	Angels that work at the planetary and galactic levels.
12th Dimension	Archangels holding universal energy frequencies.

Please note that the highest -dimensional being that we can communicate with directly is a ninth-dimensional angelic being. These are the angels that are assigned to us as our guardians, who perform miracles and, from time to time, make themselves known. In order for them to communicate with us, they are able to lower their vibration to a resonance that we can perceive through our third-dimensional frame of reference. It is actually not possible for us to communicate directly with an Archangel. Archangels hold universal energetic frequencies that are so dimensionally removed from us that we have no frame of reference for their communication. That's not to say that the Archangels do not communicate with us! Usually, however, ninth-dimensional angels will represent a specific Archangelic Realm. There are many people who feel that they are communicating directly with an Archangel. This is not technically correct. They are communicating with a representative from that Archangel's realm. This does not invalidate the quality of the information or the experience of communicating with an angel, by any means. I just believe that we should know exactly whom we are talking to. Most people do not have a frame of reference that asks a discorporate entity to identify their dimensional state. So when an angel or other upper-dimensional being presents itself from an Archangelic realm, many may interpret this to be "the Archangel Michael." Information from other dimensions will present itself through whatever frame of reference we have available to us. Now that you have a more detailed, expanded frame of reference, you can ascertain exactly what kind of entity is initiating communication with you.

If a positive entity that wishes to communicate with you is a fourth dimensional being, it is most likely an Earthbound Spirit. It is unlikely that these beings have any message of particular value, since their spiritual perspective is the same or lower than your own.

If an entity from the fifth dimension or above contacts you, you may ask them their purpose for communicating with you. They may well want to teach you something or bring you a message of great value. You may ask whether they represent an Archangel realm, or a specific spiritual council. They may wish to instruct you on a new frame of reference within which to receive intuitive information. By all means, learn all you can from these beings. Once again, have a tape recorder or writing materials handy—chances are you will not remember all the information, especially if the resonance of the entity you are communicating with is very high.

I always recommend a healthy degree of suspicion when an entity introduces itself as an upper-dimensional being. Sometimes, negative entities will pose as very highly evolved master teachers and seek to flatter you. They may claim that you have been singled out, that you are special, gifted or very highly evolved. Be wary of flattery from the spiritual realm. Positive entities do not need to flatter our egos. You should ask again whether the entity in question is in alignment with Divine Love, Light and Truth.

At no time is it appropriate to yield control of your physical body to another entity. This kind of communication, where an entity is allowed to "take over," is not only an unnecessary practice, but also not in alignment with Divine Love, Light, and Truth. It's also pretty scary! You should, at all times, have conscious control over receiving information, have a fairly decent general recollection of that information, and should be able to consciously formulate questions, just as when you are communicating with your Higher Self.

The same rules for quality of information apply to communication with these entities as it does for your Spirit Guides. Information from the spiritual plane is uplifting, enlightening, helpful, practical, and direct. It benefits the highest good of everyone. It is not cryptic, confusing, or contradictory. It does not demand obedience, or flatter your ego. Information from the spiritual plane is never intended to create glamour or appeal to a need or desire for power. Information from the spiritual plane will contain suggestions and advice, but always acknowledges the power and responsibility of free will and free choice.

I have encountered quite a few instances in which negative entities were leading my clients astray. One of my clients received mysterious riddles for years and believed that she was communicating with Spirit Guides and departed loved ones. In fact, these were negative entities posing as helpful spirits. In most cases, the information from these negative entities is just accurate enough so as to be believable. Over time, though, these entities will also relay a lot of misdirection that creates negativity, confusion and doubt. Do not abdicate good common sense in your communication with entities from the spiritual plane. Negative entities can pose as your Spirit Guides, as ascended masters and teachers, and even as departed loved ones in order to gain your trust. If information seems inconsistent or out of alignment with your personal values, or proves to be obviously inaccurate, you may wish to cease communication with the entity in question.

WHEN GRANDMA COMES CALLING

On occasion, departed loved ones may present themselves and get your attention. Before simply taking these entities at face value, please make sure once again that you are communicating with a positive entity. There are a couple of reasons for this. For one, you want to make sure that the entity presenting itself as Grandma truly is the Soul that once was Grandma. It is entirely possible for an attaching negative entity to access your subconscious memory files and create a fabulously accurate impersonation of Grandma. In this case, however, it will have to identify itself as a negative entity when you ask.

When we leave the physical plane, positive Souls cross over into the positive astrals. We do leave this plane of existence. If a recently departed loved one presents itself to you, this Soul may need assistance in making the transition. Sometimes Souls are unaware of their own passing and do not find their way. In this case, please pray for their assistance in crossing over. The spiritual organization responsible for transporting Souls to the appropriate astral plane is called the Third Order. Please request their assistance in transporting the Soul of your departed loved one to the astral plane justly earned. This will ensure that they cross over appropriately and safely, and it is a wonderful service you can provide for them. Once they have left the physical body, Earthbound Spirits do not have enough vital force to make this request themselves. They may well be contacting you for assistance.

There are many, many Earthbound Spirits within our dimension. Some of these may truly just be bored and looking for someone to communicate with. I advise that you ask them if they wish assistance in crossing over. Again, if they wish this assistance, please direct a prayer request to the Third Order to help them cross over. If they are fourth or fifth dimensional beings, I do not advise communicating with them beyond this point. Their perspective is the same as yours, and they do not have information to offer you that will help you on your Soul's path and purpose. Communicating with these entities is about the same as making small talk at a cocktail party—it may be somewhat amusing and entertaining, but has little real value to add to your life.

From time to time, the Souls of departed loved ones that have successfully completed their crossing may check in with you. After establishing that they are indeed a positive entity, you may wish to ask them their purpose for contacting you. Perhaps they need your assistance, or have a specific message for you. Once again, the guidelines for receiving appropriate information from the spiritual plane apply.

BE DISCERNING

There are a great many entities that can be valuable resources to us on our path. There are also a great many entities that may seek to actively mislead and misdirect us. Be very careful and discerning about which entities you open your lines of communication up to. Just because an entity is non-physical does not mean that it has helpful information for you. Communicate with your Higher Self and your Spirit Guides. If a spiritual master or guide contacts you, and you have identified this entity as being positive and from a believable dimension, learn all you can from this being. These entities are wonderful resources that can expand your frames of reference and allow you to access a new level of consciousness.

✆

CHAPTER EIGHT

RESOLVING INCONSISTENCIES

You are creating a strong, clear method of communication with your Higher Self so that you may accurately and reliably access intuitive information. However, there are some issues that may need to be addressed, should you encounter some inconsistencies or difficulties on your path of intuitive development. These issues may include receiving consistently conflicting answers, or an unresponsive or erratic pendulum.

If any problems arise, you should always first check that you are still connected to your Higher Self. Simply ask:

* *Am I 100% connected to my Higher Self, consciously and subconsciously at this time?*

> ◈ *Is all information coming from my Higher Self, and is the information 100% in alignment with Truth?*

These are always the questions to start with should you receive confusing or conflicting information. If you are disconnected from your Higher Self, repeat the process outlined in Chapter Two to re-establish the connection. You may ask after you complete the process once whether further repetition is necessary.

If you discover that you are fully connected to your Higher Self, but are still having difficulties receiving consistent answers through your divination method, you may be encountering environmental, emotional, or mental interference energy.

ENVIRONMENTAL INTERFERENCE ENERGY

What if nothing happens when you try to use your pendulum? What if it doesn't swing at all? Sometimes, it can seem as if a pendulum has gone a little crazy!

Usually this is because of environmental interference energy. When a pendulum is not working properly after you've followed the steps to clearing and programming it, it is a very good indication that something in your energetic environment that needs clearing. There may be some interference energy linked to your property, or the space in which you are trying to dowse. However, there may also be a restriction or negative influence in your own energy field.

Here are a few things to try:

> ◈ Change location. Try another room in your house. If you've been working in your living room or study, try a room with less electronic equipment. If that doesn't work, try going outside, or even leaving your property and try dowsing in a nearby park or other quiet public area. This is a good way to determine if the issue lies within your property.

> ◈ Try burning sage (smudging) before you start dowsing. You can obtain

bundles of sage meant for this purpose in most metaphysical and alternative health food stores. The smoke from the smoldering sage has energy clearing properties. This is a good way to clear minor interference energies in your property.

◆ Try smudging yourself by passing the smoldering sage along your body to clear your own energy field.

◆ Take a bath in sea salt and lavender essential oil. This will also clear your energy field.

EMOTIONAL INTERFERENCE ENERGY

Your method of divination seems to be working just fine, and suddenly, the answers stop making sense. What if you are connected to your Higher Self, but are still receiving conflicting answers to your questions?

It may well be, if you are working with emotionally charged subject matter, that your subconscious mind has taken over and you are no longer receiving information from the appropriate source. Instead of accessing your Higher Self, your answers are now coming directly from your subconscious, which makes them unreliable at best.

If you are heavily emotionally invested in the outcome of your questions, there may be too much emotional energy surrounding the issue to receive a clear answer. Questions such as: *"Am I pregnant?" "Is it probable that I will be laid off during my company's reorganization?,"* or *"Is it possible for me to recover from this illness?"* are all so emotionally charged that, unless you can maintain an exceptionally clear state mentally and emotionally, you may get conflicting answers or "wrong" answers.

You can double-check where your information is coming from by asking:

◆ *Is my subconscious mind currently supplying independent answers to my questions?*

◈ *Am I in the appropriate emotional state to receive meaningful and accurate information from my Higher Self in alignment with Divine Truth at this time?*

If there is too much emotional energy surrounding the issue you are asking about, you may wish to do one of the connection exercises outlined later in this chapter in order to regain a state of emotional clarity.

MENTAL INTERFERENCE ENERGY

Let's face it—sometimes we want to receive certain answers to our questions. We already have the answer we want in mind, and this prevents us from being in a conscious observer mode. Note, first of all, if your conscious mind is still merely a spectator or audience member—or if it has become the director of the play! Additionally, you can ask:

◈ *Is my conscious mind at this time creating interference energy?*

◈ *Is my conscious mind supplying the answers to my questions?*

You may also simply be tired or distracted, and unable to generate the focus necessary to receive intuitive information. In that case, ask:

◈ *Am I in the appropriate mental state to receive meaningful and accurate information in alignment with Divine Truth at this time?*

If the answer is no, put your pendulum aside and come back to your questions another time. If you wish to continue, try one of the following exercises to put aside any mental interference energy that may be disrupting your intuitive process.

CREATING CLARITY

As you become more and more accomplished in accessing your intuition, you will encounter less emotional and mental interference energy. However, if maintaining a state of emotional and mental clarity proves difficult, you may try the following exercises before you begin your divination process.

◈ Sit quietly and comfortably, and close your eyes. Allow your body to relax. Inhale through your nose and exhale through your mouth. Take one hundred breaths like this—count them internally. Let any thoughts arise within your mind without investing in them. Keep your mind engaged in counting your breath. This will prevent you from investing too much energy into your thoughts.

◈ Sit quietly and comfortably, and close your eyes. Relax your body. Breathe in and out through your nose. Observe the breath as it enters and exits your nostrils. Notice everything you can about the quality of your breath, without judgment. If your minder wanders off, simply bring your attention back to your breath, without judging yourself for losing focus. Keep coming back to observing your breath. Do this for five minutes.

◈ Sit quietly and comfortably, and close your eyes. Imagine a line of energy dropping from your root chakra at the base of your spine, all the way into the Earth. Imagine this line of energy, this grounding chord, traveling all the way into the center of our planet. Now imagine sending all excess emotional energy, all upheaval, all negativity, down the grounding chord into the Mother Earth. Allow the Earth to absorb the energy, neutralizing it. Give anything you cannot use right now to Mother Earth. Bless the Earth and thank her for assisting you in this process.

ACCURATE MISINFORMATION

Of course I rely very heavily on my intuition, not just in my profession, but also for guidance in my personal life. Over the years, I have learned to trust the information I receive implicitly. However, there is one aspect of working with intuitive information that I do find irritating, even as I completely recognize the need for it. I like to call this aspect "accurate misinformation."

Sometimes Divine Truth is the information *we most need to hear right now* in order to move us forward towards a specific path. Sometimes, our Higher Self and our Guides know that it will take a certain piece of information to guide us towards our highest path and purpose—even if that piece of information turns out to be factually inaccurate. Yes, our Higher Self is not beyond misleading us for our own highest good.

Let me illustrate with a personal example: After the birth of my daughter, I struggled with a chronic health condition that, while minor, created a great deal of disruption in my life. Many treatment options, from surgery to medications to physical therapy presented themselves. Prescription drugs offered me immediate, much-needed relief. While managing this condition with medication, I tried out a few other treatment options, including physical therapy. Using my intuition, I eventually designed my own yoga practice to correct the issue I was experiencing. All in all, I felt much better. But I was highly reluctant to go off my medication, fearing that my symptoms would return. So, while pursuing my alternative treatment plan, I stayed on prescription drugs.

One day I was overcome with the very odd impression that I might be pregnant. This was certainly not impossible, though not exactly probable. All dowsing and intuitive processes confirmed a pregnancy. It would have been too soon for a pregnancy test to yield accurate results. And so I did what any responsible woman in my situation would hopefully do—I went off my prescription medication. To my great relief, I did not suffer the return of any previous symptoms. Six days later, I discovered that I definitely was not pregnant.

Was I upset? Absolutely! Would any other information have persuaded me to stop my medications? Honestly—no. When I first began my alternative treatment plan, I had set my intention to no longer need prescription medication. But fear truly kept me from going off the drugs. And so my Higher Self gave me the only piece of information that would lead me to make the choice most in alignment with my intention, and my highest path and purpose. The possibility of a pregnancy was truly the only thing that made me do the "right" thing. So, as irritating as it was to receive factually inaccurate information, in hindsight I am grateful. Using my intuitive resources, I devised my own alternative treatment plan—under the care of my physician, who was thankfully very open-minded—and it allowed me to avoid possible surgery. And I no longer need prescription medication. Over all, this was a very empowering experience. But, along the way, I needed a big shove in the right direction from my Higher Self.

Occasionally, we receive information that, while not factual, is accurate nevertheless. It is what we need to know, in that moment, in order to make the choice most in alignment with our highest path and purpose. Our Higher Self does not mislead us, but it knows us better than we sometimes know ourselves.

THE NEED FOR PRECISION

When asking for intuitive information, nothing is more important than establishing a clear frame of reference within which to ask our questions. We have worked hard throughout this book to establish a very clear intent with our carefully worded questions. If we do not know exactly what it is that we are asking, the information we receive in response to our questions may be equally unclear. The answer is only as good as the questions we ask. Sometimes, in spite of our best efforts, our frame of reference here in the physical does not match that of our Higher Self on the spiritual plane.

Let me illustrate with another example. I was preparing to teach my Professional Intuitive Training Class, and I dowsed to discover how many students I might expect to sign up. It's an intense class that takes a lot of my time and energy, and I like to have between five and eight students in the course. I was told that six students would sign up, with a 100% probability. Four days before the start of the class, only four students had signed up. I was a little puzzled by this—I'm used to receiving highly accurate information. Two days before the class, no additional students had signed up. Then I received an e-mail from one of my students who had already registered. She was concerned about any energetic shifts that might occur during the class, since she was pregnant with twins.

I had a good laugh when I read this e-mail—here were my two additional "students." Energetically, these two little Souls would certainly be present for the class, and undergo all attunement processes together with their mother. So, from the perspective of the spiritual plane, they would certainly be students in the class.

Obviously, I didn't ask the right question. If I had asked what the number of *"paying students"* or the number of students *"currently in a physical incarnation"* would be, I would have certainly received a different answer.

If you find yourself receiving what looks like a wrong answer, check in with how your frame of reference may be perceived on the spiritual plane. This is where a log or diary of your questions may come be particularly handy. You may find that you have been given the right information, after all.

TRUST YOURSELF

Remember that your intuition works flawlessly. It was just a matter of developing a clear and precise method of conscious access. Your intuition has been guiding you throughout your life, whether you've been aware of it or not. The information you receive will resonate with you as truthful on a very deep, instinctive level. This is ultimately how you measure your own accuracy. The methods outlined in this book are designed only to bring forth what has been yours all along. You are the expert of your life. Allow your inner wisdom to shine forth.

℘

EMBRACING YOUR HIGHEST PATH AND PURPOSE

There is no better time than today to develop your intuitive skills. Having an clear and reliable line of communication to your Higher Self is an invaluable resource. Your Higher Self is your ally in creating a life that truly expresses who you are. Your Higher Self and your Spirit Guides will assist you in aligning with your highest path and purpose, in the big and small choices that shape all your life experiences. My hope is that this book has given you a means to access the fullness of your resources on the spiritual plane.

As you align more fully with your highest path and purpose in all aspects of your life, you will find that your overall level of satisfaction and fulfillment increases. Your life will suit you perfectly, and allow for your gifts to blossom. When inner alignment spans all planes of existence, from the physical to the spiritual, there is truly nothing that you cannot achieve.

My blessings to you all,
ANDREA HESS

RESOURCES

For a free companion workbook to all the exercises presented in this book, please visit www.EmpoweredSoul. com/workbook.htm.

Discover more about the author's work and intuitive development resources at www.EmpoweredSoul.com. To contact Andrea for personal appointments or to schedule an *Unlock Your Intuition* book event or workshop, please call 480-471-5688 or email her at Andrea@Empowered Soul.com.

If you are interested in professional intuitive development through the Soul Realignment Practitioner Program, please visit www.EmpoweredSoul.com.

Printed in the United States
204436BV00002B/395/A

9 780979 637704